THE KENYA CERAMIC JIKO

The Kenya Ceramic Jiko
A manual for stovemakers

HUGH ALLEN

INTERMEDIATE TECHNOLOGY PUBLICATIONS in association with
APPROPRIATE TECHNOLOGY INTERNATIONAL and CARE
1991

Intermediate Technology Publications
103–105 Southampton Row
London WC1B 4HH, UK

Appropriate Technology International
1331 H Street NW
Washington, DC, USA 20005

CARE
660 First Avenue
New York, NY, USA 10016

© AT International and CARE 1991

ISBN 1 85339 083 6

Appropriate Technology International (ATI) implements its mission with public funds made available through the Agency for International Development. ATI's programme is carried out in co-operation with the Office of Rural and Institutional Development within AID's Bureau of Science and Technology.

A CIP catalogue record for this book is
available from the British Library

Typesetting by Inforum Typesetting, Portsmouth
Printed in Great Britain by Short Run Press, Exeter

Contents

FOREWORD vii
ACKNOWLEDGEMENTS ix
1. Introduction 1
2. Some production issues 4
3. Costs and prices 10
4. Making the metal case 13
5. Ceramic research 31
6. Producing the liner 41
7. The kiln 56
APPENDIX A Use and care of the jiko 73
APPENDIX B Engineering drawing set 75
APPENDIX C Names and addresses 99

This book is dedicated to Rafat Gabbani of Omdurman, Sudan, Rafiki Juvenal of Gituza, Rwanda, Mohammed Majzoub of CARE Sudan, Kamwana Wambugu of Tigoni, Kenya, and Sally Westwood of CARE Rwanda, all of whom either make or promote the Kenya Ceramic Jiko (KCJ).

Foreword

The Kenya Ceramic Jiko, known locally as the KCJ, is a charcoal-burning stove, now manufactured not only in Kenya, but also in Sudan (Canun El Sarour), Uganda (Ceramic Sigiri), Rwanda (Canamake), Tanzania and Togo (Asuto). To a more limited degree it is made also in Malawi. It consists of a ceramic liner fitted inside a metal case. Compared to traditional metal stoves made in these countries, it burns 25–40 per cent less charcoal. In almost all cases it is made by private entrepreneurs.

It is difficult to obtain reliable production figures for each country where the KCJ is made, or even from individual manufacturers. But in Kenya, monthly output is believed conservatively to be about 4500–5000 stoves (although some estimates are as high as 11,000,[1] I believe the lower figure to be more realistic). In Sudan, where the stove was introduced in 1986, approximately 800 stoves are being made per month.

Overall in Africa monthly production stands at a minimum of 8000 units, and is expected to rise dramatically within a short time. These 8000 KCJs save up to 180,000 tonnes of fuelwood annually (t/pa) that no longer needs to be converted into charcoal. In typical use the stove saves about 25kg of charcoal per month. Since 6kg of firewood are consumed in making 1kg of charcoal, this represents a saving of about 150kg of wood per month per user, or 1.8t/pa. A stove lasts about 1 year, so 8000 sold monthly will result in 100,000 stoves in daily use. This in turn may lead to annual savings of wood of more than 180,000t. These are simplified statistics, but in the author's view represent a reasonable estimate. While fuel-saving technologies are no substitute for reforestation, they are an important complementary activity. How much money would need to be spent to create managed plantations able to provide a sustainable fuelwood tonnage that approaches these economies?

Although this manual does not directly address this issue, it illustrates a cheap and profitable technical process for making the KCJ, a stove which is already bought by the thousands every month and contributes significantly to national energy savings.

The potential market for the stove in the countries where it is manufactured is several times larger than at present. There is a huge unexploited opportunity to introduce it not only to many other countries in Africa, but also in Asia and Latin America.

The purpose of the manual is two-fold:

○ to list the conditions that make manufacture and use of the stove both desirable and possible, and, conversely, to list conditions that make it impractical; and
○ to show how the stove is made.

The manual does not try to prove the superiority of the KCJ compared to other stoves. Its success in the market is sufficient endorsement, and other written materials discuss its comparative efficiency.[2]

The manual suggests a particular approach to ceramic technology employed in making the stove. It recommends semi-mechanized production that requires fairly significant levels of investment (US$5000–20 000 total investment per production unit). This is not only intended to encourage larger volumes of output, but to establish proper standards of technical quality.

The ceramic technology described was developed in Kenya between 1986 and 1988 by A.T. International (ATI) and CARE. It is now also used in Uganda, Sudan, Togo and Rwanda, where CARE has stoves programmes. ATI is introducing the stove in Senegal.

The KCJ appears to be the most popular of many charcoal-burning stoves being tried out

1. Jones, H. Mike: *Energy Efficient Stoves in East Africa*, Report No. 89–01 of the Office of Energy, USAID.

2. For an assessment of the merits of ceramic-lined jikos *vis à vis* other alternatives see 'The Economics of Improved Charcoal Stoves in Kenya', Eric L. Hyman, *Energy Policy*, April 1986, and 'The Strategy of Decentralized Production and Distribution of Improved Charcoal Stoves'. *World Development* 15(3), March 1987.

in Africa, based on the numbers sold and the willingness of private, small-scale artisans to make it. It is popular with users primarily because of its fuel economy and safety in use.

It has been widely and easily adopted because it is modelled after the Kenyan traditional metal stove (TMS) design and requires no change in methods of cooking or stove use. Other improved stoves are nominally more efficient, but none is as easy to use (An example is the UNICEF UMEME with a PHU (percentage of heat used) efficiency of about 34 per cent compared to 32 per cent for the KCJ and 17 per cent for the TMS. The UMEME needs a specially sized pot to fit the stove which limits its usefulness and consumer appeal. It uses less metal in manufacture than most alternatives and lasts up to three times as long, since there is much less oxidation of the metal components.

The biggest barrier to its widespread manufacture lies in the difficult commercial marriage of metal and ceramic technology. For this to take place there must be co-operation between potters and metalsmiths and trust among small-scale artisanal producers, as well as agreement concerning acceptable standards of product quality.

The majority of existing stove manufacturers are metalworkers. Although they work co-operatively among themselves, they are not used to relying on inputs from other informal-sector producers. Their links are mainly with the formal sector, which supplies scrap metal and semi-manufactured inputs. The character of the relationships between potters and stove-makers will determine if the KCJ can be produced independently and sold in a given context. Governments and NGOs need to design creative programmes that encourage these relationships.

This manual is intended to provide some guidance in promoting the KCJ, and to demonstrate a method of production which has been successful in Africa in the last four years. I hope it will help in similar efforts elsewhere.

Hugh Allen
Maseru
June 1990

Acknowledgements

This manual has been made possible by a collaborative effort between A.T. International (ATI) and CARE International, both of whom have contributed to the technical development of the stove, and to programmes in East and West Africa that promote its adoption and use.

Larry Frankel, my supervisor at CARE, is to be thanked for his willingness to fund and support this work 'sight-unseen'.

Arleen Richman, of ATI for supporting this work and for editing the manual; thanks also to Eric Hyman of ATI for his suggestions, and to ATI for co-funding this publication.

Davidson Njoroge's drawings make this a far shorter and much clearer manual than it would otherwise have been. This job has become far more complex than envisaged originally and I am indebted to him for his patient creativity.

Robert Kinyua, of Gordon Melvin & Partners, is responsible for the drawings of the moulding machine, which were done at short notice.

Nick Evans, also of Gordon Melvin & Partners, has been encouraging and enthusiastic about the engineering drawing work which he has supervised.

Mike Bess, of Bess Associates, has provided commentary, insight and encouragement, not to mention usable advice which kept our work in Sudan and Rwanda on a practical track.

CHAPTER 1

Introduction

The development of the Kenya Ceramic Jiko (KCJ)

The KCJ has developed over the last eight years as a result of work carried out by the Kenya Renewable Energy Development Project (KREDP), a USAID-funded project in Kenya, implemented by Energy Development International (E/DI) through the Ministry of Energy.

In 1981, Keith Openshaw of KREDP brought a Thai Bucket stove to Nairobi. The apparent simplicity of the design and dramatic fuel savings were impressive, and it was quickly agreed to try and adapt it for use in Kenya. A study tour was organized to visit sites in Thailand where several thousand Bucket stoves are made each month. These sell on the streets of Bangkok and other Thai cities for about US $1.00 each. Although produced in many different sizes and in different forms, the various Thai stoves share a number of features:

o They consist of a bucket-shaped metal case, fitted with a liner. The gap between the casing and the liner is filled with rice-husk ash and sealed with cement.
o They all have removable 'throw-away' grates.
o The pot rests directly on the rim of the ceramic liner.

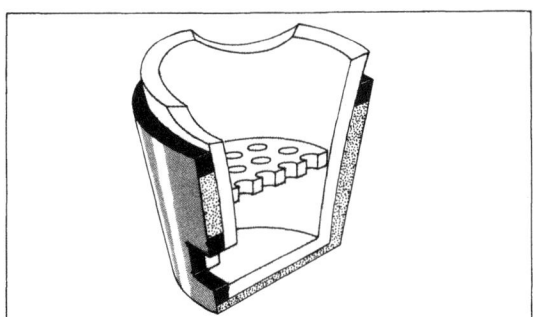

Figure 1.1: *Thai Bucket stove*

In 1982, assisted by stoves advisor Maxwell Kinyanjui, KREDP began work to develop a Kenyan version of the Thai stove. Initial experiments with cylindrical liners were disappointing. The first prototypes included an extruded cylindrical liner with a separate grate inserted into a traditional Kenyan metal stove. With that design, the ceramic liner was prone to crack and it was difficult to fix firmly in the metal cladding. This showed that the tapered shape of the Thai stove served two purposes:

o It prevented collapse of a cracked liner inside the casing. If the liner cracked, gravity would hold it in place under slight pressure against the sloping metal shell.
o A sloping fit allowed the liner to expand and shift within the metal casing. A ceramic liner formed as a cone segment and fitted inside a similarly shaped metal case converts horizontal expansion into a slight vertical shift of the liner within the case.

KREDP, however, felt the bucket design was inappropriate for Kenya. The narrow base of the stove made it inherently unstable and a likely cause of accidents in the kitchen (many types of Kenyan food require vigorous stirring). Surveys indicated that this was a basic consumer concern. (KREDP involved consumers in the process of stove design and acted on their views.)

Accordingly the stove casing was modified to the present, waisted, shape, giving the stove one of its currently popular names: bell-bottomed jiko. The second prototype consisted of a flat-bottomed, conical liner, set below the rim of the cladding, with the pot resting on metal supports built into the rim. This was known as the full-liner stove.

The main difference between the tapered ceramic liner used in Kenyan stoves and those of Thailand is in the wall thickness. In Thailand, the liner is commonly 40–50mm thick; in Kenya 20–25mm thick. The reason for this change is not clear, but was probably intended

Figure 1.2: *First bell-bottomed full-liner stove*

to reduce weight and cost. The Thai Bucket needs to have a thick liner, because the pots stand directly on pot-rests carved into the clay. In Kenya the pot sits on metal supports attached to the case. This reduces the need for strength in the ceramic liner, and does not affect its efficiency. The use of metal pot-rests was recommended by users.

In early designs, a ceramic grate was made as a separate piece from the ceramic liner. This permitted easy replacement of a single part which has a tendency to burn out. However, it was found that having a separate grate significantly increased the rate of cracking of the liner as a whole.

An important modification, a half liner, introduced at this point enabled the stove to become a viable product for consumers and producers. A half liner combined with the bell-bottom shape provides greater stability, costs less, reduces cracking rates of liners and weighs less (thus is more portable) than full liners. The half liner, which does not continue below the level of the grate, is the type of liner still produced. It consists of a tapered ceramic insert with an integral grate, cemented into the metal case using a mixture of vermiculite and cement.

Properly made half liners will last for several years. If the liner cracks or the grate fails (after about one year), the rest of the stove is still usable and can be refitted with a new liner. To date, liners have been outlasting the casings. A TMS in average daily use needs to have its metal grate replaced every 3–4 months; the casing rusts through within a year.

Figure 1.3: *Current bell-bottomed half-liner stove, the KCJ*

The final modification made to the Thai design was to install a tightly fitting airgate. Various types of Kenyan meals need high, rapid heat, while other foods are simmered. The airgate allows the stove to be operated in both high- and low-heat modes, and this contributes significantly to improved fuel economy.

The development of the KCJ from the Thai Bucket shows that changes are usually needed to transfer technology from one country to another. Although the stove dimensions and shape of the KCJ are identical in Kenya, Sudan, Rwanda and Uganda, the size of the pot-rest differs to accommodate local styles and methods of cooking; for example round-bottom pots. In Togo, where consumers desire a thicker metal, hammer dies and spot welding are used instead of the production method described in this manual.

Development of manufacture and sales

It was assumed that within a short time the stove would be available throughout Kenya. It would be produced in myriad small workshops by metalworkers who purchased ceramic inserts from village potteries and the like. By mid-1984, four producers were supplying the Nairobi market with ceramic liners. The liner manufacturers ranged in size and capability from well-organized factories with relatively sophisticated equipment to backyard workshops that produced only a few dozen liners per week. All of these liner manufacturers, however, were competing mainly for the Nairobi market. Very little had been done to supply outlying smaller markets nor to promote the interests of village-based artisans and potters, a situation that continues to this day. The intense competition for the important Nairobi market has reduced the price of the most popular liner by 60 per cent over the last 6 years from KSh35 to KSh12. This is a drop of 81 per cent at 1983 prices. While this competition benefits consumers it inhibits new investment in expanded production.

To accelerate the commercial production and sale of the bell-bottomed jiko outside Nairobi, ATI approved, in mid-1985, a three-year grant to the Kenya Energy Non-Governmental Organizations Association (KENGO), which continued the work that had begun under the USAID KREDP project.

The ATI project was to provide training and technical assistance to enable 20 informal-sector manufacturers of traditional jikos throughout Kenya to produce the improved ceramic-lined stoves. In addition, support was provided for development of better methods of clay processing, moulding and firing, publicity and public education campaigns, a marketing programme and a quality-control certification process. Because it is very difficult for small workshops to obtain credit from formal sources, a small loan-fund was set aside to provide capital to assist existing potters to build kilns and buy equipment for the production of jiko liners.

To increase the availability of improved jikos, at a price affordable by poorer households, the ATI project adopted a decentralized production strategy that relied on existing informal-sector metalsmiths and potters. Although the ceramic-lined stove gained in popularity as the price was lowered, the early results were disappointing: the quality of the ceramic liners was not uniform; faulty liners, which adversely affected the stove's efficiency and durability, threatened to give the stove design a bad reputation; and production figures were much lower than anticipated.

ATI decided to experiment with upgrading one producer's activities by partially mechanizing the production of liners. As the ATI staff engineer assigned to the project, I designed a motorized moulding machine, known as a jigger-jolley (the conventional name by which this machine is known in the ceramics industry), which increases the production rate and the uniformity of moulding, and reduces cracking rates substantially. This single intervention transformed the producer, Waka Ceramics, from a marginal operator supplying 5 per cent of Nairobi's demand into a major competitor. Although introduction of the jigger-jolley and other improvements reduced quality-control problems substantially, and expanded production, the cost of this equipment limited production to a few medium-scale enterprises. Contrary to ATI's original intentions, it is likely that liner production in Kenya will be dominated by a few medium-size firms in Nairobi and a few other areas such as Mombasa, Kisumu and Nyeri. Decentralized liner production appears possible only in areas where there is a living tradition of pottery making; this is not the case in most parts of Kenya.

Waka Ceramics and the technical package

In 1986, Kamwana Wambugu, the headmaster of a primary school, was one of several small-scale liner-makers, producing about 120 KCJ liners per week. Three months later, thanks to the use of the jigger-jolley, he was producing and selling more than 400 liners every week.

Cracking in drying had been reduced from 30 to 10 per cent, solely as a result of using the machine. After changing the clay mixture and drying process, such cracking was later eliminated. Not only were the liners of better quality, they looked smooth and strong. Because the liner is made with the right materials and properly fired to the right temperature, it continues to sell.

The jigger-jolley was still in operation in 1990. New moulds allow it to make three different sizes of liners, using a single forming blade. Wambugu rarely sells less than 1500 liners per month and he has established a reputation for quality that sets a high standard for other liner-makers.

Wambugu's profits have been ploughed back into his business. His first major investment was to construct an updraught kiln, able to hold 450 liners at a time. He then invested in a pugmill and finally a pulverizer (two useful pieces of equipment that are not essential). Other than the jigger-jolley, which was financed by ATI, all equipment has been built by CARE at Wambugu's request, and at his own cost. This steady development has guaranteed him a thorough understanding of the technical process and the management demands associated with each.

Lessons learned

The manual attempts to share the insights gained from working with Wambugu in Kenya, and in Sudan. The three cardinal principles for making a KCJ can be summarized as follows:

o There is no substitute for good quality materials. It takes time to develop the right clay mixture. Even the best machines cannot compensate for a bad clay body, and customers are the first to react.

o A KCJ liner-maker must have a well-designed, economical kiln, which fires quickly and evenly.

o Although good quality liners can be made by hand on a potter's wheel, the jigger-jolley significantly improves output, appearance and durability of the finished liner. In starting a stoves project in an area/country where demand has not been established, it may be better to begin *limited* production on a potter's wheel before investing in a jigger-jolley. When upgrading the business, however, a jigger-jolley is the first machine that should be built, even in simplified form.

CHAPTER 2

Some production issues

Under what conditions is it possible to produce the KCJ? Before we describe how to make the KCJ, we need to decide if it is desirable to produce the stove. Bear in mind that burning charcoal, even in an improved jiko, consumes more net energy than wood combustion. When charcoal is burned in a KCJ, you get only half the amount of heat that would result if you burned the amount of wood needed to make that charcoal.

Charcoal is a partially burned wood, produced in a process where air is excluded from the fire. This causes extremely slow, partial combustion, and turns the wood into the carbon that we know as charcoal. A lot of the stored energy in wood is used to make the charcoal.

Although charcoal consumes more net energy than wood combustion, it is a preferred fuel in towns and cities because:

○ it is light, (it only weighs ⅙–⅛ the weight of the original wood) and cheap to transport;
○ for its weight and volume it produces a lot of heat, so you need to store a smaller volume of fuel; and
○ it burns without smoke, which makes it easy to use anywhere in the house or in houses without fireplaces.

Before promoting the use of the KCJ, the NGO or private entrepreneur should determine if there are better alternatives. For example, promoting the KCJ as a modern stove in very small, rural settlements where fallen wood is readily obtainable might increase the overall local demand for wood (to be made into charcoal), as well as consumer costs for energy. In these places, it might be better to promote the construction of woodstoves and use of fireplaces in low-cost housing than to establish a charcoal stove business. The questions to ask when deciding whether to promote the KCJ are:

○ Do alternatives to charcoal exist?
○ Do these alternatives reduce the overall demand for wood?
○ If so, are these alternatives cheaper for consumers? If not, are there simple ways to reduce the cost?

Only if the answer to each of the above questions is no should attention be turned to producing the KCJ.

Size of the potential market – the issue of quality

Some stove experts believe that very small scales of production are possible and that micro-industries can be set up near even the smallest markets to make both the liners and metal casings. Data indicate a potential market of about 200,000 stoves per year in the rural areas of Kenya, half the projected urban total.[1]

The potential entrepreneur, however, needs to remember that a rural population is much harder to reach and more spread out in comparison to urban markets. Each local producer has a harder time selling stoves than his urban counterpart because the potential customers are dispersed throughout a larger area, and transport is difficult. Rural consumers tend also to be more cautious about buying a new and untried product, especially since usually they can collect their own firewood at no cost.

KCJs in the countryside largely result from urban distribution. Retailers and small-market entrepreneurs take regular shipments of finished stoves from the city to up-country towns and village markets. While small manufacturing units exist outside Nairobi, their aggregate production is probably no more than 10 per cent that of Nairobi's output.

It takes time and a considerable investment to produce a good quality liner. CARE worked nine months in Sudan, one year in Rwanda and a year in Togo before developing clay mixtures and manufacturing technologies that produced durable liners. Rather than invest the time needed to set up a liner-making enterprise in a rural area, it is probably better to create links between liner producers in the cities, who have made the necessary investment in research and quality, and small-scale metalworking artisans

---

1. Jones, H. Mike, (see p. viii), data extrapolated from Kenya Central Bureau of Statistics *Rural/Urban Household Energy Consumption Survey* (October/November 1978 and August 1980).

in rural townships. Often an introduction is enough. In Kenya, three producers in towns to the north of Nairobi make periodic trips to the city to buy their month's supply of liners.

Similar arrangements have been fostered in Sudan, where there is an established tradition in many industries of semi-manufactured inputs being transported great distances.

CARE's strategy is to target larger urban markets where the costs of charcoal are rising rapidly and to encourage distribution of finished and semi-finished stoves to outlying towns and villages.

CARE's experience in Rwanda suggests that a city or a market town of 200,000, whose lower and middle-income inhabitants rely on charcoal as a cooking fuel, is the minimum size of market in which to apply this technical package on a commercial basis.

Even with an aggressive sales campaign, the initial rate of market penetration for a city of this size will be no more than 10 per cent in the first year. In a sub-Saharan African city of 200,000 approximately 30,000 households may cook with charcoal. To achieve a 10 per cent penetration rate a business must sell 3000 stoves a year, or 250 a month.

What conditions make it possible to produce the KCJ?

Material requirements

Two basic materials are needed to make the KCJ: clay and metal. These materials must be found close to the production sites and markets.

Metal: The stove casing is made from mild sheet steel, although galvanized material is used sometimes if suitable supplies of scrap are not available. All the joints in the casing are either riveted or folded, and no welding, soldering or brazing is required. The production method in this manual presumes that metal sheet (most likely scrap) is available.

A thinner steel can be used in the KCJ than in the TMS because the ceramic liner protects the metal from direct contact with the burning coals, and rusting is slowed. The double cone shape of the casing provides inherent strength,

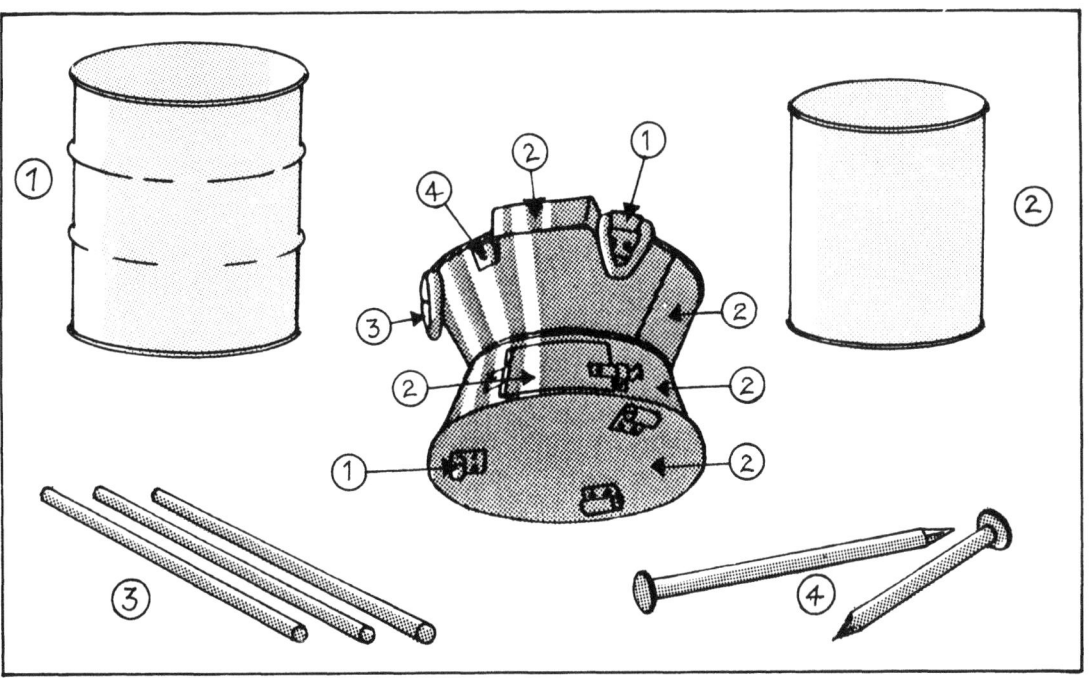

Figure 2.1: *Materials used in making the KCJ casing*

which is reinforced by insertion of the ceramic liner. A good source of mild sheet steel is scrap bitumen drums. Oil drums are made from metal which is thicker than necessary.

The minimum recommended thickness of sheet for the casing is 0.5mm, and the thickest is 0.8mm.

The entire stove can be made from this material, with the exception of the pot-rests, feet and pot-rest holders. The pot-rests should be made from mild steel roundbar, 7–8mm in diameter, and the feet and pot-rest holders from mild steel sheet at least 0.8mm thick, but preferably 1mm. The pot-rest holders are subject to higher tensile loads than other parts of the casing, and may tend to unfold if made from thinner material. The base of the stove is often made from even lighter steel, usually materials rejected by factories that produce tins for the canning industry. This material is about 0.25mm thick, which is sufficient since the base of the stove is protected by an insulating layer of cement and vermiculite, which prevents oxidation.

If material thinner than 0.5mm is used in the main casing, the folded joint around the waist will crack and separate after a short time. If material thicker than 0.8mm is used, making the folds and the waist joint will be awkward and difficult.

Some countries (such as Togo) prefer thicker materials, since their traditional all-metal stoves usually are made from steel plate 3–6mm thick. The material chosen for the KCJ in Togo is 1mm sheet steel. Since scrap materials are not available in Togo, the casing is formed in simple hammer dies, and joined with spot welds. This is an entirely different method of production than that for the KCJ.

In Kenya, mild scrap sheet steel is the material of choice. It is obtained from discarded bitumen drums, which are 0.5mm thick. The pot-rest holders are made from 200 litre oil-drum scrap sheet, which is much thicker than bitumen-drum steel (usually 1.0mm). The major seams are formed by folding; this is a traditional airtight method of joining galvanized household durables such as buckets. The pot-rest holders, feet, airgate and carrying handles are joined to the stove by means of rivets, made from 3–4" nails, cut short about 5mm from the head. Figure 2.1 illustrates the various materials used in making the metal casing.

In most places in Sudan, Uganda, Rwanda, Tanzania and Kenya the KCJ is made from scrap sheet steel. If scrap is not available, and new sheet steel cannot be obtained easily, it is impractical to make the KCJ; the lack of raw materials also implies an absence of skilled artisans used to working with sheet metal.

Although sheet steel and scrap may be available, price can vary widely from place to place. One of the major stovemakers in Kisumu, Kenya's third largest town, cuts out sheet-metal parts in Nairobi and sends them to Kisumu by bus, because the price of scrap in Kisumu is double the cost in Nairobi. Factors of this sort will influence the production and assembly location of the KCJ.

Clay: The availability of the right clay is the most critical factor in determining if the KCJ can be made. Clay is among the most abundant and common of all minerals, and is found in all but the harshest of climates. It is chemically described as a hydrated alumina-silicate, having an ideal chemical formula of $Al_2O_3+2SiO_2+2H_2O$. The water ($2H_2O$) is chemically combined, and takes a different form than water that can evaporate naturally from the clay. This chemically combined water is known as water of composition.

Clay is formed from the decay of igneous rocks, and is among the most varied of minerals. Clays which have decayed on the site without erosion taking place are usually the purest, and fire to high temperatures. Often white in colour, these are known as primary clays. China clay is of this type. Usually primary clays lack plasticity, but can be added to other clays to raise the melting point of the mixture.

Most clays are found far away from the site of their original decomposition. The grains of material have been carried by rainwater runoff and streams until the flow of water slows enough to deposit them. The further the clay is found from its source, the more plastic it usually is. Material of this type is called secondary or sedimentary clay.

Secondary clays are also mixed with other minerals, most commonly iron oxide, which gives the reddish colour to fired-clay products such as bricks and tiles. Clearly, the composition will reflect the almost infinite geological and geographical influences which produced the clay, and 'sedimentary clays will vary as much as the conditions that produced them can vary'.[2] Heavily contaminated secondary clays

2. Cardew, Michael: *Pioneer Pottery*, London: Longmans 1969.

are unsuitable for liner-making because when fired to even a low temperature they tend to crack and become extremely dense and brittle.

The more plastic the secondary clay, the more it tends to shrink when drying. Clay is made up of billions of flattened microscopic particles (platelets). When clay is wet, water is found between the particles. When the clay dries, the water evaporates and the platelets lie closer together. Clay can shrink as much as 15 per cent going from a wet plastic state to dry.

Clay with a very high shrinkage rate is unsuitable for liner-making because it will tend to crack when drying. This occurs because the external surface of a thick clay liner will dry and shrink more quickly than the inside, which remains damp. Adding sand, sawdust or rice-husk ash to the clay can correct this problem, but a clay that shrinks more than 12 per cent in its untreated form should be rejected.

It is worth searching for a good clay with ideal characteristics. The fewer additional materials that have to be mixed with the clay, the lower the production costs, and the less supervision is required. The best type of clay to use in liner-making can be described as follows:

o it has good physical strength when fired to 900°C, similar to the strength of a good quality flowerpot;
o it remains slightly porous when fired to 1150°C, increasing weight by more than 10 per cent when soaked in water;
o it does not warp when fired to 1250°C;
o it fires to a light colour, between pink and white;
o it shrinks less than 8 per cent going from a plastic state to dry; and
o it is plastic.

If you find a clay with all these characteristics, you have found a material that is usually classified as a fireclay. A fireclay may be described as a secondary clay from which impurities have been leached by weathering.

Since it is difficult to find a fireclay, different clay types are usually mixed, and sand, sawdust and other minerals added to form a suitable body (see pp. 33–5).

At this point, is is more important to note these additional guidelines:

o Deposits must be extensive, covering at least 2500 sq. m (50 × 50) to a depth of no less than 50cm. If the deposit is smaller it cannot be considered a dependable supply.

o Deposits must be accessible and occur close to the surface. Topsoil more than 2m deep makes mining expensive and difficult.
o No more than 50 per cent sand should be present in the clay's natural state.
o Clays must shrink no more than 12 per cent from wet to dry.

If clays which meet these general criteria are unavailable, it is probably not practical to consider making the KCJ. CARE's Sudanese project encountered this problem. Despite three year's work in El Obeid, a desert town some 500km southwest of Khartoum, no extensive and regular beds of clay could be discovered. Production of the KCJ in El Obeid is now supported by the commercial supply of liners from Khartoum.

Labour requirement

Metalworkers: Generally the stove will be made from light sheet steel by skilled artisans, who use techniques of folding and riveting to join the components. These skills are quite common, and used to make such products as watering cans, chicken feeders, water tanks, TMSs, metal suitcases, trunks and simple oil lamps. Soldering and welding skills are not needed to produce the standard KCJ. However, the type of labour and skills needed will depend on the type of casing-material preferred by consumers. For example, in Togo where thicker steel casings are the norm, a semi-formal sector metalsmith who can use hammer dies and spot-welding equipment is the leading producer.

Experience in the promotion of stoves in Haiti, Togo, Uganda, Rwanda and Sudan confirms that a competent metalsmith can make high-standard stove casings following two or three days training, if supervision is available. A trained metalsmith working alone can make 4 or 5 casings a day after a week and up to 12 a day after a few months.

The drawings of casing manufacture included in this manual are not necessary if a well-made KCJ is available to serve as a model. Most metalsmiths are more comfortable copying a physical example than reading even the clearest set of sketches.

Clayworkers: No special skills are required to make the ceramic liner if the jigger-jolley is used. Wambugu, for example, uses several unskilled labourers. If the capital is not available to finance a jigger-jolley, skilled moulders can make a high-quality liner, as can potters trained in the use of a potter's wheel. In Thailand, good quality liners for the Bucket stoves are produced on potters' wheels; neither the jigger-jolley (nor the pugmill) is part of the technology process.

The business owner must understand the materials employed and their processing, both in terms of manufacture and end-use. In addition, the owner must be familiar with the working, management and maintenance of any equipment.

The experience of small-scale turnkey projects in Africa, where a process and a plant is bought as a whole, is depressingly uniform. It may be summarized as: 'Fine, until the first breakdown/change in raw materials/shift in market demand.' Those industries that have grown by natural stages where the owner understands thoroughly both the business issues and the technology involved, have the best long-term prospects for growth and the means to cope with changing conditions.

If the industry is too small to afford professional technology management, it is important that the owner understand the nuts and bolts as well as the balance sheet. Kamwana Wambugu cannot read an auditor's report, but he can read the temperature of his kiln by eye, a vernier micrometer, and the trends in the market. He acts on all of that information. A ceramics workshop demands more technical management skills than a sheet-metal shop, because there are more variables.

Good quality technical management in the production of the ceramic liner has been taken as a must. Where it did not exist, the projects have failed.

Market strategy
The minimum size urban market in which to introduce the KCJ has already been suggested — 200,000 people, or approximately 30,000–40,000 households. There are increasing numbers of towns approaching this size throughout the world, and many of them depend on charcoal as their basic cooking fuel.

How can the stove be introduced to the consumer?

In Kenya, the Shauri Moyo open-air market has made dissemination of the KCJ comparatively easy. Shauri Moyo is not only a production site but a retail/wholesale market. (Shauri Moyo is Nairobi's major informal-sector production centre. As many as 400 metalsmiths produce a wide range of household goods, including the KCJ.) Assembly and sale are controlled largely by the individual metalsmiths. Apart from a few large orders from government, the market is fragmented. Wambugu has a shed at Shauri Moyo, staffed by a saleswoman. He drops off his liners twice a week, notes the trend in sales for large, medium or small liners, and adjusts production plans accordingly. Wambugu has benefited from KREDP's intensive promotional efforts; by the time he started production, the market for KCJs already existed.

CARE's experience in Sudan and Rwanda has been entirely different. In both countries the stove was previously unknown and there was no easy penetration into a mass market. In each case CARE adopted a strategy of initiating production through a technical entrepreneur who was an established potter and had some limited experience in producing ceramic stove components. The rationale was as follows:

o there was a proven demand for the stove;[3]
o technical assistance was expected to be more effective when provided to an established and competent manufacturer;
o existing producers would be able to work through retail channels in order to establish the KCJ as a credible product in the market; and
o established producers possessed the commercial and entrepreneurial skills necessary to organize the manufacture of other inputs (casings or liners) from outside sources.

In Togo, CARE has chosen to work with a metalworker for the same set of reasons. The guiding criteria were: technical competence; entrepreneurial ambition; willingness to invest; and willingness to be responsible for marketing. In Togo there was no well-established pottery company that met these conditions.

In every case from the outset CARE has asked that producers define and implement a sensible marketing strategy. The explicit contract between CARE and the business has involved:

---

3. In Khartoum the Sudan Renewable Energy Project (SREP), funded by USAID through the Energy Research Council, had field-tested 400 KCJs. CARE's decision to promote the stove, and upgrade its technical quality was made on the basis of SREP's survey work. Mary Clarkin and Brad Tyndall, *Improved Charcoal Stoves for the Sudan*, Energy Research Council, July 1986. This report concluded that consumers liked the KCJ more than either of the other stoves tested.

- the owner assuming total responsibility for production and sales;
- CARE being responsible for the commissioning and introduction of the needed technology; and also a public information campaign, consisting of radio, television and newspaper advertising, feature articles and the like, timed to coincide with the introduction of the stove; and monthly/bi-weekly pay days!

Generally mass-media campaigns are more effective than market demonstrations and attendance at trade fairs which reach only a comparatively small group of people. (Attendance at fairs is good business after the stove is well-known.) Posters are effective if they are used in conjunction with mass media and to identify sales outlets. A logo, used throughout all media promotions, helps in product identification — right down to stickers attached to each stove.

Figure 2.2: *Example of stove logo used by Wambugu as a sticker*

Figure 2.2 is an example of a sticker Wambugu uses on stoves fitted with his liner. A similar sticker is used in Sudan as a form of quality control. Stickers inform buyers that the stove is approved by the Sudan Energy Research Council, and are given to the stove-maker only after a current batch of stoves has been inspected. In the early stages of promotion this is an effective way to build consumer confidence in a new product and to ensure good quality production at the enterprise level.

It is useful to offer a guarantee, which allows the liner to be replaced without cost up to at least three months after purchase. This option is rarely exercised by the consumer, but is a useful confidence-building measure and alerts producers to long-term quality problems. If a significant number of stoves from a particular batch is returned, it points to deviations in material quality or production methods.

There is no inflexible sales doctrine, at least not in Africa where marketing systems vary tremendously. In West Africa, for example, there is a highly organized system of commercants, who are basically a cartel of wholesalers, responsible for just about everything that is bought or sold. It is wise to work through this system, since there are few alternatives. On the other hand, in Sudan it is practical to deal directly with wholesalers and retailers. After an initial effort involving weekly visits to some 40 retailers, the shopowners and wholesalers started to come to the Khartoum factory, which now only accepts trade orders for a minimum of 100 stoves.

CHAPTER 3

Costs and prices

Costs

Most very small informal-sector businesses arrive at a product price by determining the costs of materials and adding whatever they think can be charged to cover the cost of labour. This is fine for an artisan whose only investment is a set of tools that cost the equivalent of a few dollars. Small informal-sector businessmen usually know their direct production costs to the nearest cent; then they bargain with customers to reach a price that gives them a wage for the day. If they need to replace tools and cover unforeseen expenses, they usually borrow money from friends and family. There is no need to worry about rent, taxes and licence fees. It is a rare informal-sector metalsmith who stocks raw materials and finished goods beyond those needed to operate for a few days at a time.

As we have seen already, a pottery-maker/liner producer either has to supply liners to metal artisans or make a complete stove. Either way, he must deal with a different set of commercial realities than the small informal-sector artisan. A much higher level of investment is tied up in the cost of premises, machinery and equipment, raw materials and a large amount of work in progress. The informal-sector artisan has only direct costs to consider; that is materials and the cost of labour hired to help complete a particular job. The only fixed cost is the cost of living.

A more organized business has to consider two types of cost — fixed and variable. Fixed costs *must* be paid, even if there is no production — rent, for example. Variable, or direct costs, change as levels of production change. A good example is raw materials. In assessing the costs of production the business owner should divide the calculations into these two categories, starting first with variable costs.

Because it is difficult to estimate the amount of material, time and labour needed to make one stove, a pottery maker will find it more practical to estimate the manufacturing costs of 100 stoves, or the costs incurred over a two-day period of production. In Kenya, variable costs for one firm in 1989 are listed in Table 3.1.[1] (At the time the rate of exchange was KSh18.5 = US$1.) KSh25.76 have to be spent on materials, labour, fuel and firewood for one stove. However, this figure excludes fixed costs.

Fixed costs must be allocated equally to each stove. If the level of production is low, fixed costs are allocated over a small number of stoves and the fixed cost per stove is high. If production is high, the share of fixed costs charged to each stove will be small. Businesses with low fixed costs can adapt to changes in sales better than businesses with high fixed costs.

To return to our example, let us look at the fixed costs of the business (see Table 3.2). Because there are on average 22 working days in

Table 3.1: *Variable costs to make 100 KCJ stoves (2 days production)*

Clay purchase price	320kg @ KSh120/t	38.40
Labour: moulders:	@ KSh2 per liner	200.00
claymakers:	2 @ KSh30 per day	60.00
Firewood	65kg @ KSh550/t	35.75
Electricity		15.00
Metal casings	100 @ KSh18 each	1800.00
Cement	63 stoves per bag @ KSh85	134.90
Vermiculite	120 stoves per bag @ KSh80	66.65
Paint	24 stoves per litre tin @ KSh30	125.00
Transport to market	2 trips at KSh50 fuel	100.00
Total variable costs for 100 stoves		2575.70
Variable cost per unit (VCU)		25.76

1. Tables 3.1–3.3 are used to illustrate a method of costing and pricing and are not intended to indicate the actual cost of the stove.

the month, and we need to calculate fixed costs for two days, we divide the monthly fixed costs by 11. We then divide the result by 100, the number of stoves we expect to make in two days, to get the fixed cost per stove made during this period.

Table 3.2: *Fixed costs per month (in KShs)*

Rent	1200.00
Foreman	1973.00
Office expenses	800.00
Repair and maintenance	500.00
Depreciation of machinery @ 15% pa	3300.00
Loan repayments (KSh55,000 @ 15% over 3 years)	1907.00
Total monthly fixed costs	9680.00
Fixed costs for 2 days (9680/11)	880.00
Fixed costs per unit (880/100)	8.80

Table 3.3: *Total production cost per stove*

Fixed costs	8.80
Variable costs	25.76
Total	34.56

Three points need to be noted:

○ If production drops to 50 units in 2 days, half the original anticipated production, the fixed costs charged to each stove will double, from KSh8.80 to KSh17.60, increasing production cost to KSh43.36. Therefore it is highly desirable for the business to operate at a high capacity use rate.
○ Two of the more expensive costs are depreciation and loan repayments. It is important to include both of these costs in arriving at a price for the stove.
○ The stoves that are produced must also be sold. There is no point in having an efficient production system operating at full capacity if marketing is neglected. Without sales, the business will go bankrupt.

Pricing

In determining the price for the stove the business owner must consider several factors: the price of alternative and competing stoves; the managerial salary (the draw); profits; and the money to be reinvested in the business.

For our example, let us say that the businessman believes that KSh45 would be a competitive market price for the stove. Producing 100 stoves every two days, or 1100 a month, should result in the outcome shown in Table 3.4.

Table 3.4: *Projected profit and loss statement*

Monthly income @ KSh45 × 1100 stoves	49,500
Monthly expenditure (fixed and variable costs @ 1100 Units per month output)	38,014
Excess of income over expenditure	11,486

The business owner can now decide if this level of earnings is sufficient to meet his needs for income and savings.

If there is no known competitive market price, the situation is different. The owner knows that the stove will cost KSh34.56 to produce and that the business is able to produce 1100 stoves per month. The owner wants a salary of KSh9500 and also wants to save KSh3500 every month to expand the factory, making a total need for KSh13,000 profit per month. Price will then be calculated as in Table 3.5.

Table 3.5: *Price calculation (in KSh)*

Monthly expenditure (fixed and variable costs)	38,014
Planned monthly profit	13,000
Total income required	51,014
Total anticipated sales — 1000 units Price (51,014/1100)	46.37

In introducing the stove into a new market with no competing product, it would be wise first to see if customers are willing to pay this price for a new type of stove. This can be determined either by sample marketing or physical demonstrations. Of the two methods sample marketing is more reliable, but this requires pilot production.

Unfortunately, it is hard to gauge reactions to the stove after a short demonstration period. Very often people are frightened by the price, especially if they are uncertain about the benefits. You may *say* that the stove will pay for itself in just three weeks but most customers will not want to wait that long just to be sure. It may be better to put stoves in homes, and in small roadside teahouses and restaurants, where follow-up is easy and people can observe their use. Early stove sales in Sudan rippled out around the homes of women who were the first buyers. After only a few days, neighbours were convinced that the stove was a better stove, and a wise purchase.

A new producer should either plan to start sales in areas where the stove is known, or plan for a relatively slow increase in the market. If the stove is only one of many products made by an established business it is easier to allow sufficient time for the stove to become known.

CHAPTER 4

Making the metal case

Size and critical dimensions

The KCJ can be made in various sizes. Other than the very large units designed for institutional use, the stoves have been the same height. This is because the grates all have a common depth, even though the diameter may differ. Too great a depth of grate will lead to either: too much charcoal being put in the grate in order to bring the burning coals close to the pot; or the coals burning too far below the surface of the pot. In either case there will be a loss of efficiency.

In practice the depth of grate for the common range of KCJs varies from 70–100mm, depending on manufacturer. Only minor differences have been observed in performance, which may be caused by other factors. We recommend a range of 70–85mm. Choosing a grate depth of 70mm means that the visible surface of the grate is 70mm vertically below the rim of the liner. (These are finished dimensions, after the clay has been fired, which may be as much as 10 per cent smaller than the liner at the time of moulding. Allowing for this is discussed in Chapter 6.) The liner is set 3–4mm below the rim of the metal case, and the grate and wall are 20–25mm thick. This means that the vertical height from the rim of the stove casing to the centre waist is 93–96mm. The total height of the stove is 200mm, with an extra 10mm added by the legs which are attached to the base of the stove.

The rim diameter of the finished stove varies in Kenya between 250mm and 310mm, with the most popular size measuring 280mm. These are diameters of the metal casing and not the ceramic liner. Diameters of the ceramic liners are always about 15mm smaller. The sizes of liner given here can be produced in the jigger-jolley moulding machine detailed in the Engineering

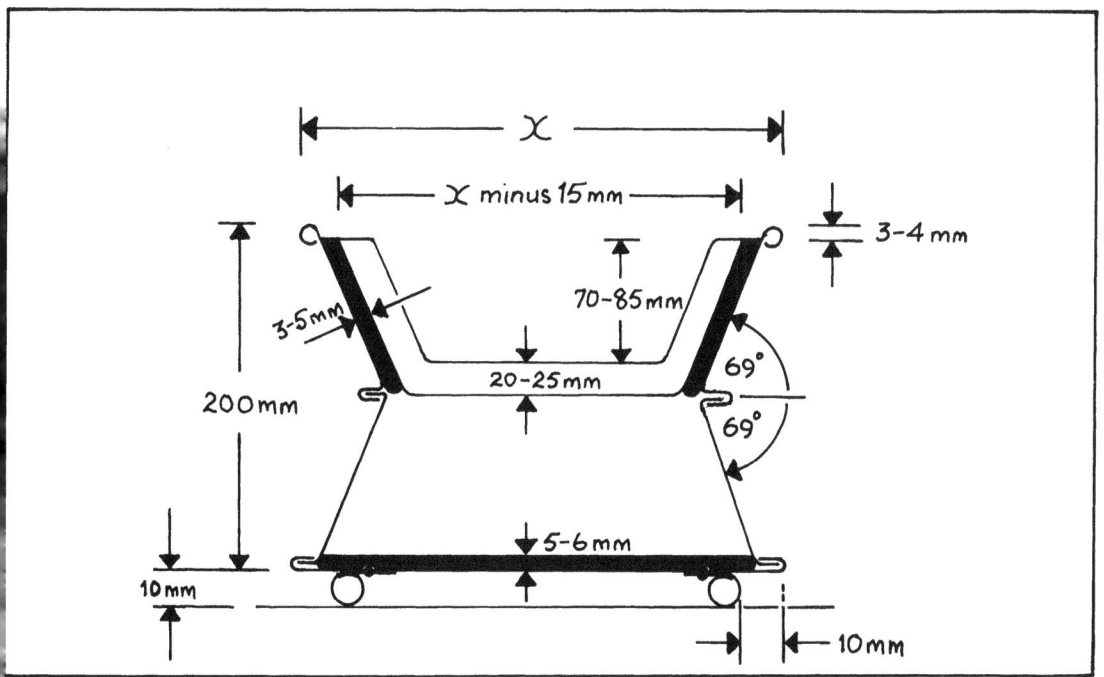

Figure 4.1: *Typical stove dimensions*

Tools

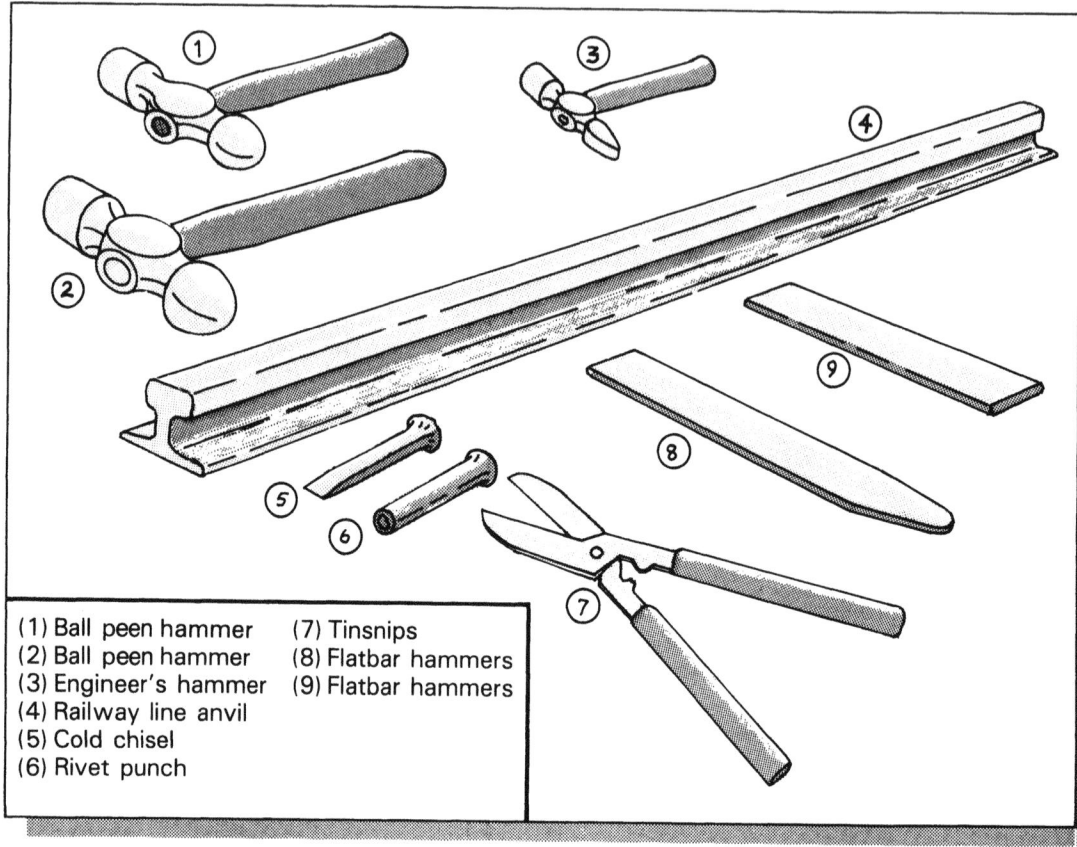

(1) Ball peen hammer
(2) Ball peen hammer
(3) Engineer's hammer
(4) Railway line anvil
(5) Cold chisel
(6) Rivet punch
(7) Tinsnips
(8) Flatbar hammers
(9) Flatbar hammers

Figure 4.2

Drawing Set (see Appendix B) (jigger-jolley is the name by which the moulding machine is known). This size is based on a clay shrinkage rate of 7.5–8 per cent from wet to dry and through the firing. If your clay has a different rate of shrinkage, an allowance has to be made in the moulds for this. The diameter of the stove will depend on local cooking needs. For example, in Sudan and Ethiopia there is a demand for a 400mm-diameter stove in which to cook wide, thin cakes (*kisrah*). In Senegal, it seems that most demand exists for the very smallest stove. In deciding what size stove to manufacture, the diameters will be determined by such local preferences.

It is reasonable to suggest that a stove with a rim diameter of less than 200mm will have only limited market appeal. On the other hand, while demand may exist for very big stoves, it is difficult to make a ceramic liner for a stove of more than 400mm diameter. Larger sizes require a general increase in liner thickness and depth, increasing the risk of cracking in use.

Figure 4.1 shows a typical KCJ in section, and gives known dimensions and angles for different sizes of stove. Where the dimensions vary (in the diameter according to stove size) they are given the value of x.

In Figure 4.1, the angle of the casing from the horizontal is specified as 69°. The angle can stray a few degrees from this recommended pitch, but it must be exactly the same as for the ceramic liner. When the angles differ the liner will touch the casing either at the top or the bottom, and will not be gripped evenly over its whole surface area.

Whatever dimensions are chosen for the stove, it is important that the liner-maker be involved as early as possible. It is expensive to make moulds for the moulding machine (in Kenya they cost the equivalent of US$120 each). In contrast, metalsmiths can cut templates from scrap in 10 minutes.

If the potter is given the desired dimensions of a liner it is possible to make moulds that produce it within a few millimeters accuracy.

Once the fired liners are available, templates can be cut by the casing-maker which conform precisely to the size and slope of the liner, leaving room for the joining cement.

Tools

Figure 4.2 shows a typical set of tools used by a sheet-metal worker in Shauri Moyo, Nairobi. They are similar to the tools found in workshops all over Africa, and can accomplish an astonishing range of work.

Apart from hammers, which are store bought, all other tools are either recovered from scrap or forged locally. The only tools that receive any sort of special treatment are the cold chisel and the rivet punch, both of which are best made of high-carbon steel. They are hardened by heating to a cherry red, and plunged through a 10cm thickness of waste oil into cold water.

The cost of a complete set of tools ranges between KSh600–800 (US$30–40), and constitutes the majority of capital invested in fixed assets. An artisan will usually erect a temporary shelter; the better organized will have a stock of goods in process and inputs such as scrap metal and liners. Considerable working capital can often be tied up in these supplies. Some artisans will have a more sophisticated range of equipment, such as simple mechanical punches, forges with mechanical fans, blacksmith anvils and specialized hammers for forming dishes.

It is tempting to look at the tools and conclude that metalsmiths of this class are all pretty much the same. This is not so; there is a wide variation of skill, investment and work organization. A typical KCJ-maker probably employs at least one assistant, divides up the work into specialties, and may even subcontract with other producers for parts or complete casings.

The tools shown here are a comprehensive range and not all are essential. The most important are the engineer's hammer (3), railway anvil (4), cold chisel (5) and rivet punch (6). Although the cold chisel can be used to cut out sheet, the tinsnips should also be considered indispensable. The flatbar hammer is made from a vehicle leaf spring, which is extremely hard.

Templates

Efficiency and standardization in the manufacture of any sheet-metal product require the use of templates. Templates are patterns, usually made of sheet metal, cut to the exact shape of the parts. They are used to mark out the shape of the stove components on fresh sheet steel, and are made from thicker metal than the parts themselves so that they will last a long time and not be mistaken for work in progress.

Templates should be made from material at least 3mm thick. It is hard work to cut and shape sheet metal of this gauge, but the precision and consistency that templates bring to the final product justifies the effort. Remember, whatever errors exist in the template will appear repeatedly in the finished stove. It is better to spend time on the template than in continually correcting badly shaped parts.

Do not use existing stove components as templates. If templates are improvised in this way, inaccuracies will creep into the finished work.

The templates shown (see Figure 4.3) are sufficient to make the entire stove, with the exception of the base which is marked by scribing with metal compasses. The number of parts needed to make a single stove is noted in brackets after each piece. For example, template 1 is intended to be used to form the main body of the stove for which four parts are needed. There are two carrying handles, and template 4 is used to mark both of these parts. Template 7 is used to cut out not only the pot-rest holders but also the feet of the stove. These parts are also formed to the same shape.

Different gauges of metal are used. Table 4.1 indicates the range of thicknesses that are acceptable for each part.

Table 4.1: *Gauges of mild sheet steel used in the KCJ*

		mm
1	Casing	0.50–0.8
2	Air door (gate)	0.25–0.8
4	Carrying handles	0.50–0.8
5	Air door latch	0.50–0.8
6	Air door latch hook	0.50–0.8
7	Pot-rest holders and feet	0.80–1.0
	Base (not shown)	0.25–0.5

Templates & Number of Pieces Needed to Make 1 Stove

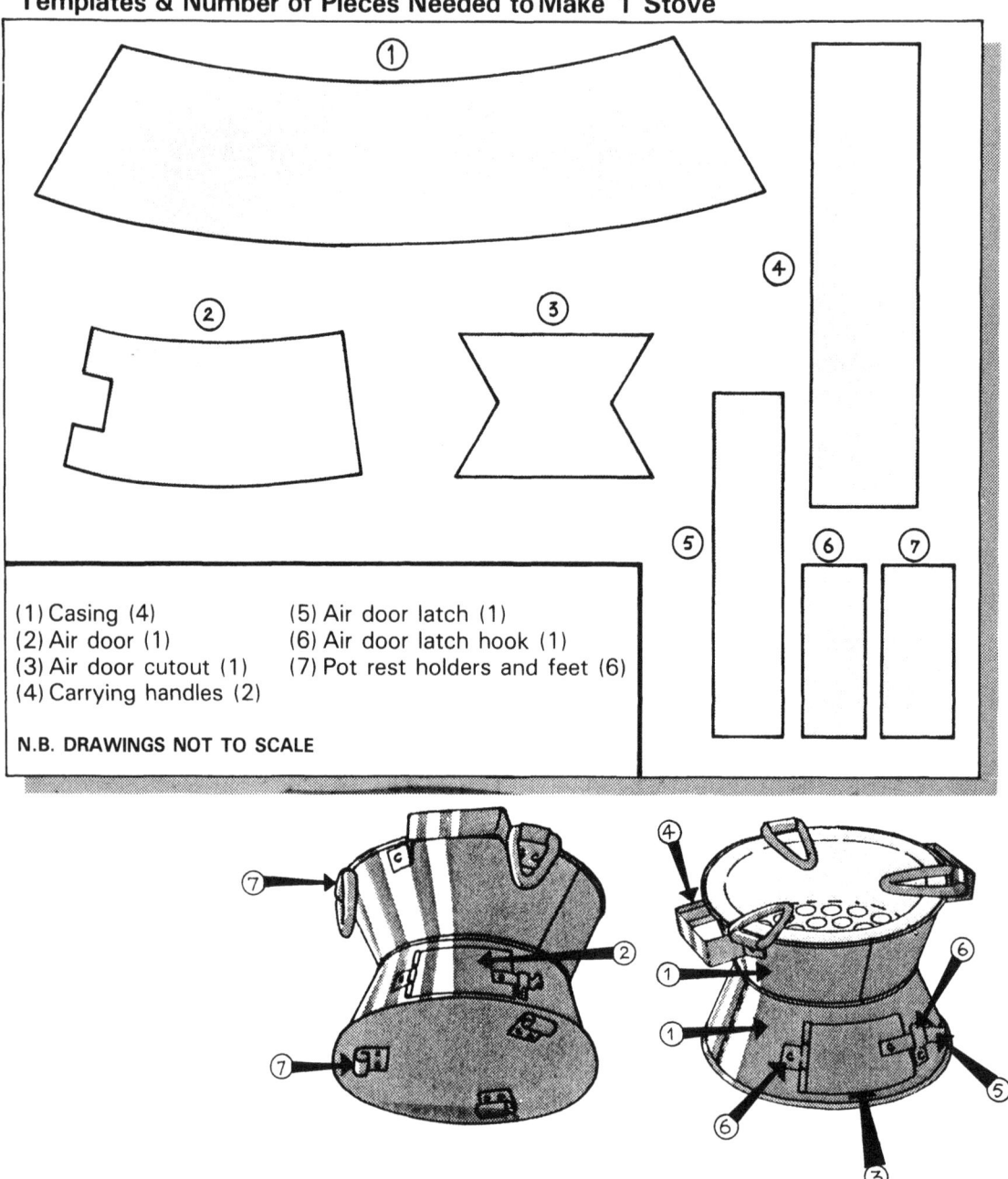

(1) Casing (4)
(2) Air door (1)
(3) Air door cutout (1)
(4) Carrying handles (2)
(5) Air door latch (1)
(6) Air door latch hook (1)
(7) Pot rest holders and feet (6)

N.B. DRAWINGS NOT TO SCALE

Figure 4.3

Riveting

Although the body of the stove is assembled by using folded joints, all the supplementary parts are attached by means of rivets. If good quality rivets can be obtained at an affordable price, they should be used, but it may be cheaper and more practical to convert nails into rivets. This is done (see Figure 4.4) by using a sharpened cold chisel to cut the shank 5–6mm below the head. The nails most commonly used are between 3" and 4" in length (7.5–10.0cm), and make ideal rivets since they are made from soft mild steel, which is relatively ductile and yet quite strong.

It is not appropriate to use pop rivets (a commercially available rivet in which the shank of the rivet is expanded by pulling a steel pin through the hollow rivet body) for four reasons:

Riveting

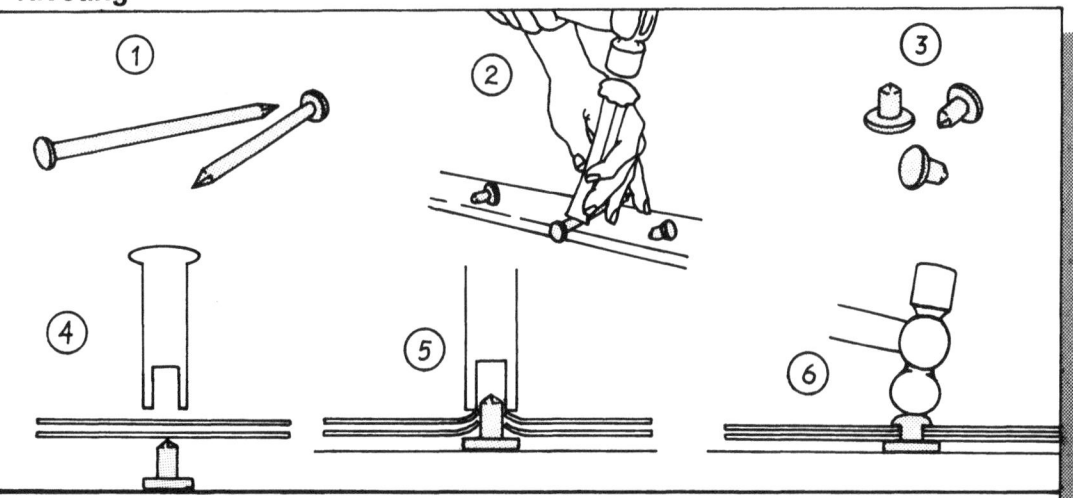

(1) 3" or 4" nails
(2) Cutting nails to size
(3) Nails as rivets
(4) Rivet placed below sheets to be joined, with rivet punch in position.
(5) Rivet penetrates both sheets when punch is hit with hammer.
(6) Closing rivet with hammer to join sheets.

Figure 4.4

o they are hollow and made of aluminium, and are much weaker than nail rivets;
o they protrude a long way on the inside of the work, making it hard to fit the liner;
o they make it necessary to drill the casing (nail rivets can be punched straight through the case); and
o they cost more.

Instead of drilling holes to receive the rivet, a special rivet punch can both drill the hole and set the rivet in place. This requires the following steps:

o The two pieces of sheet to be joined are placed immediately above the nail rivet, which is set on the anvil (see Figure 4.4(4).
o The metal is lightly tapped with a hammer so that the nail indents the metal. This shows the metalsmith exactly where the rivet is resting, and confirms that the location is correct.
o The rivet punch is placed over the indent, so that the hollow centre of the punch is directly over the shank of the rivet. It is struck smartly with a hammer. This punches the rivet through both sheets of steel.
o The rounded end of a ball peen hammer is used to spread the head of the rivet and to firmly join the two parts.

Using this method a rivet can be located and fastened in less than 15 seconds.

Marking, Cutting and Preparation of Casing Material

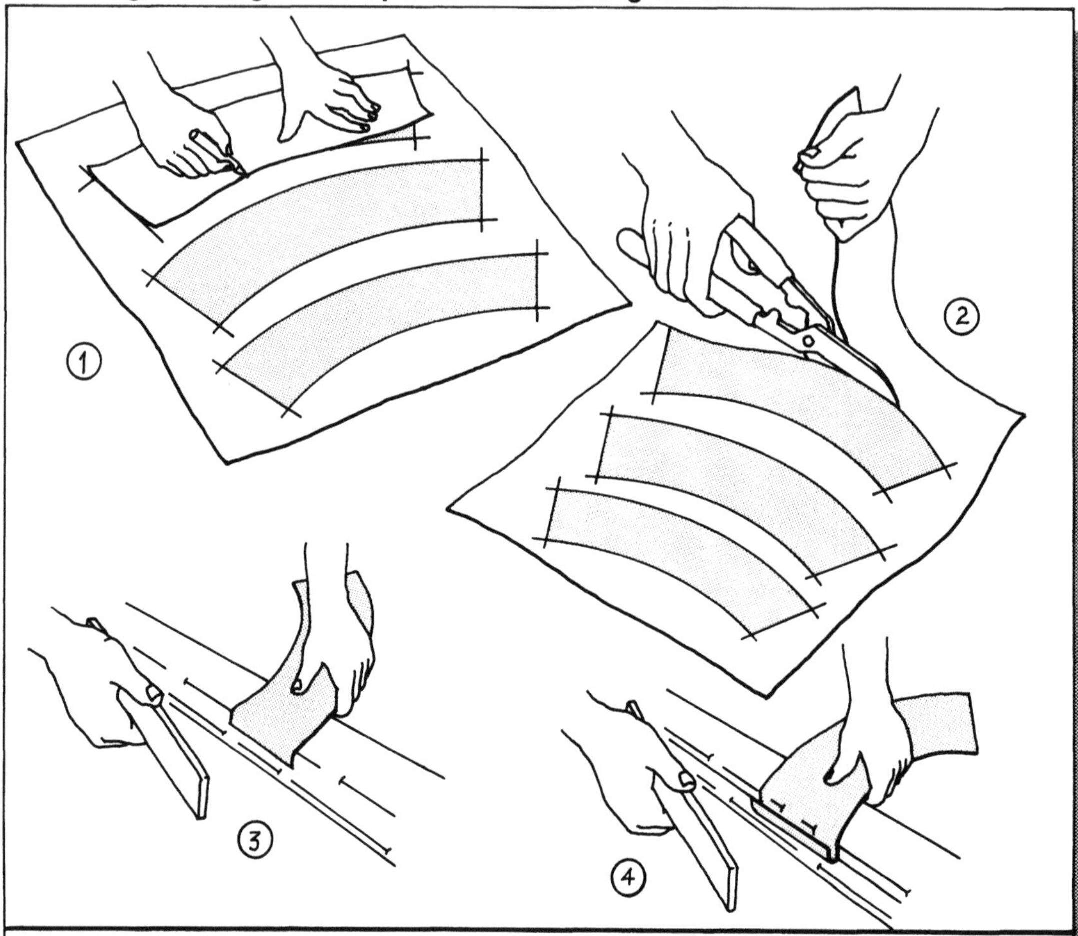

(1) Marking using template
(2) Cutting out
(3) First bend for joint
(4) Second bend for joint

Figure 4.5

Marking, cutting and preparation of casing material

Figure 4.5 shows material being marked, cut and folded for use in making the KCJ case. As already indicated this is made of sheet steel and should be 0.5–0.8mm thick.

To save material, each half of the casing is made in two parts. If it is cut as a single piece as suggested by some observers up to 30 per cent fewer stoves can be made from a sheet of scrap metal.

Figure 4.5(1) shows the template being used to mark the outline of the casing material. Although, in the interests of clarity, the parts are shown spaced apart, in practice they will be much closer together in order to avoid wasting material. The template is shown with the corner raised to clearly illustrate that it is made from a separate piece of metal. In practice the template should be flat and smooth.

Marking out is best done with a scriber so that the surface of the metal is scratched. While a pencil can be used, it is not as accurate. An excellent scriber can be made from an old hacksaw blade, ground to a point.

Figure 4.5(2) shows the tinsnips being used to cut out the casing material; (3) and (4) show how the railway line anvil and a flatbar hammer are used to prepare the folds which join the two half-casing pieces. A flatbar hammer has the advantage of bending the entire length of the metal at once, rather than in short stages. This makes the work go more quickly and contributes to a better finished appearance.

Joints prepared in this way are a standard means of joining sheet metal, and widely used to make such items as buckets and watering cans. They are usually used to make a watertight joint. They are exceptionally strong and they provide a rib on opposing sides of the half-casing to give it extra rigidity. The drawing of the completed stove in Figure 4.5 shows the

Preparation & Assembly of Half-casing

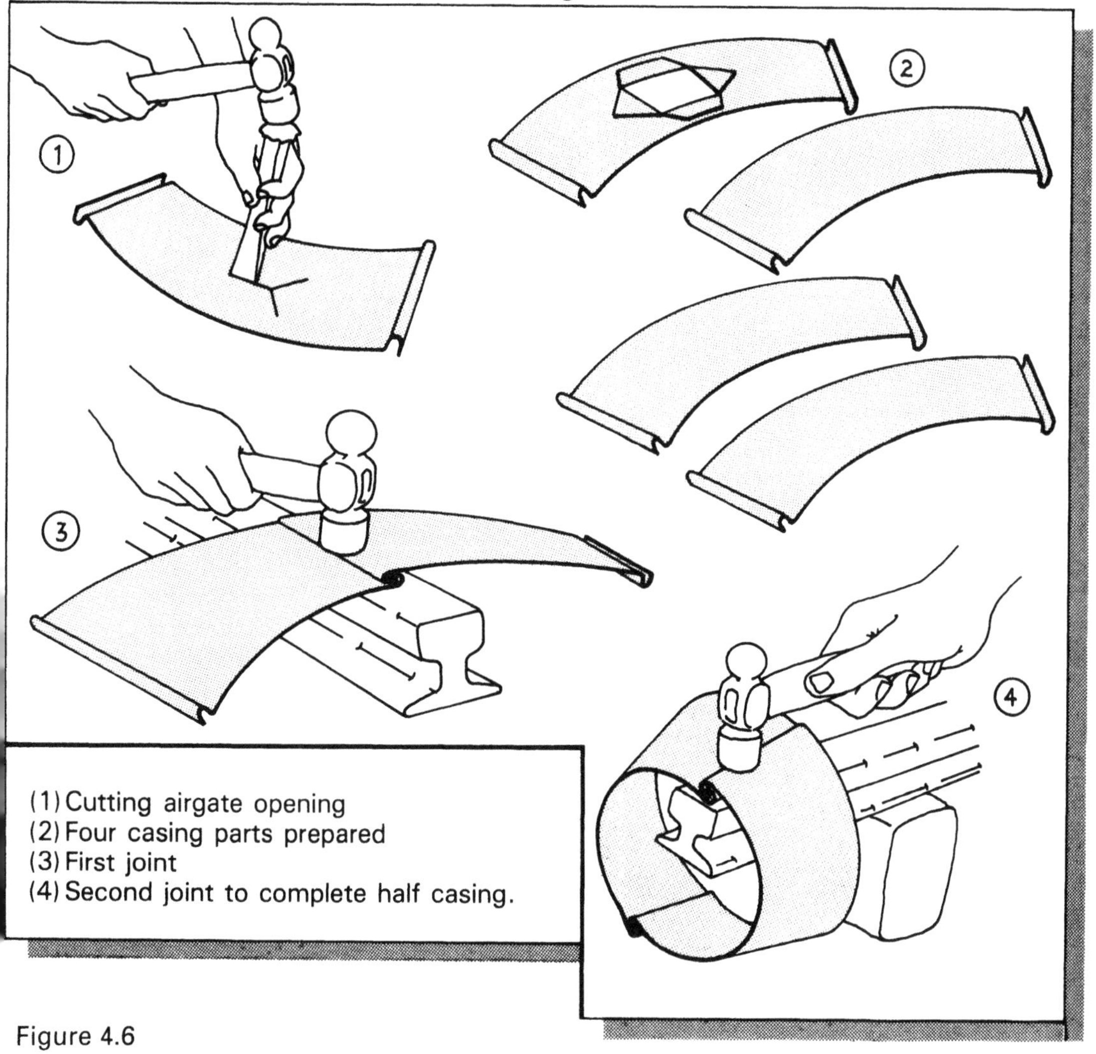

(1) Cutting airgate opening
(2) Four casing parts prepared
(3) First joint
(4) Second joint to complete half casing.

Figure 4.6

four casing components. It can be seen that the joints on the upper half of the stove are set at 90° around the circumference of the stove to the joints on the lower half. Again, this arrangement contributes to an increase in stiffness.

Preparation and assembly of half-casing

Before the half-casing is assembled the airgate opening has to be cut in one of the casing parts. Since the four casing parts are identical until this point, any one can be selected to receive the airgate.

Figure 4.6(1) shows the opening for the airgate being cut with a cold chisel. This cutting follows marks which are scribed using template 3 (see Figure 4.3). This process is not shown here. When the opening has been cut by the chisel the edges are folded back as shown in Figure 4.6(2).

Using the railway line anvil two of the half-casing pieces are joined to make a flat continuous curve. (If the pieces are incorrectly joined they will form an S shape.) This is done by linking the folds at the ends of the half-casing pieces and hammering flat. A properly made joint of this type will be airtight, extremely rigid and exhibit no looseness. This is shown in Figure 4.6(3).

Figure 4.6(4) shows the completed half-casing being joined into a continuous conical band. When this process is complete you will have made the two casing halves. They will be identical except that one will have a rectangular hole for the airgate. It is important to remember that the airgate belongs to the lower half of the stove.

Until this point, the only difference in the way the casing halves are made is in the airgate opening. From now on the halves are treated and formed in completely different ways.

At this time the open ends of both casing halves should appear even and level. If the bell-shaped open ends are rested on a flat surface, any irregularities will be visible as gaps between the rim of the casing half and the surface.

Preparation of joint between upper and lower casing halves

The joint between the upper and the lower halves of the stove casing is the most difficult to prepare, because the space in which to work is restricted.

Figure 4.7(1) shows the preparation of the lower half of the casing. This part is hammered on the upper and lower rims to make horizontal flanges, about 3–4mm wide, at both the wide and the narrow ends of the casing half. Figure 4.7(3) shows the two halves. That on the left with the airgate hole shown becomes the lower part of the stove. The sectional drawing on the left shows how the bends in the casing look when viewed from the side, that is with two similar flanges at the upper and lower edges.

Figure 4.7(2) shows the preparation of the upper half. A flange is made at the narrow end of the casing half in the same way as in (1), but slightly larger, about 6–7mm in width. When the flange is complete it is folded into a cupped shape as shown in (3) as a section on the right side. The other end of the casing is curled around on itself to make the top rim of the stove which *must* be even and level.

When preparing the two casing halves, remember that the waist flange on the lower half must fit very closely inside the cupped waist flange on the upper half. If not, it will form a weak joint.

Preparation of Joint Between Upper & Lower Casing Halves

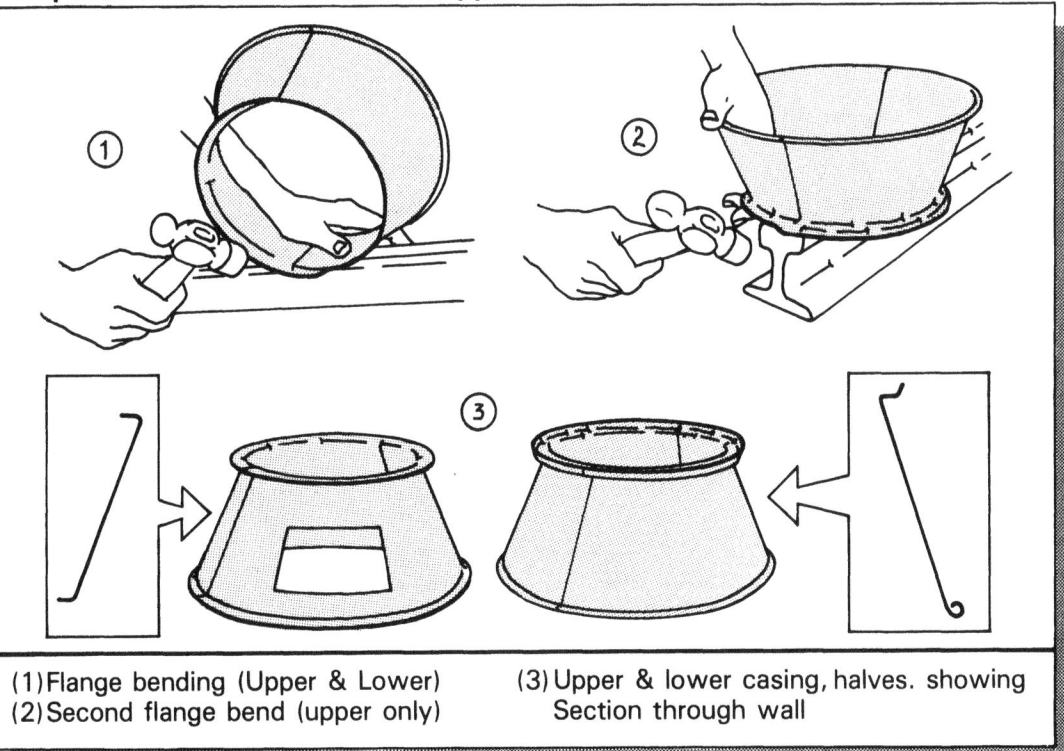

(1) Flange bending (Upper & Lower)
(2) Second flange bend (upper only)
(3) Upper & lower casing, halves. showing Section through wall

Figure 4.7

Joining casing halves

Figure 4.8(1) shows how the two halves are placed together and how closely the two parts must fit. There must be enough material on the upper half to permit further folding to securely grip the flange on the lower casing half. When the casing halves are joined the seams which form joints in the casing halves are put at 90° to each other. Throughout this whole operation, it is important to support the work on a rail anvil.

Figure 4.8(2) shows the flange in the upper half initially being hammered around the flange in the lower half.

Do not attempt to make the joint tight by using the hammer in this way.

If you do, the joint will end up being loose, and you will make a series of dents in the lower half of the casing. Stoves made in this way will fall apart after a short time in use. This is the single most common mistake made by new casing-makers.

Figure 4.8(3) shows how this joint is securely closed, using the chisel-shaped tail of an engineer's hammer, while the inner part of the joint is supported on the anvil. This closes the seam completely, makes for a strong joint and avoids unsightly dents. When the joint is made, ensure that the top and the bottom are still level, and have not been distorted during this operation.

Despite the fact that the casing is made from very thin material, the double-cone shape ensures an extremely rigid structure. At this point a man weighing 100kg should be able to stand on the casing without causing any deformation. Unfortunately, this also means that if the rim is oval or uneven in a vertical direction, there is little chance of correction. It is vital that the stove-maker keeps an eye on the roundness and evenness of the casing throughout.

At this point it is too late to make major changes in the casing.

Joining Casing Halves

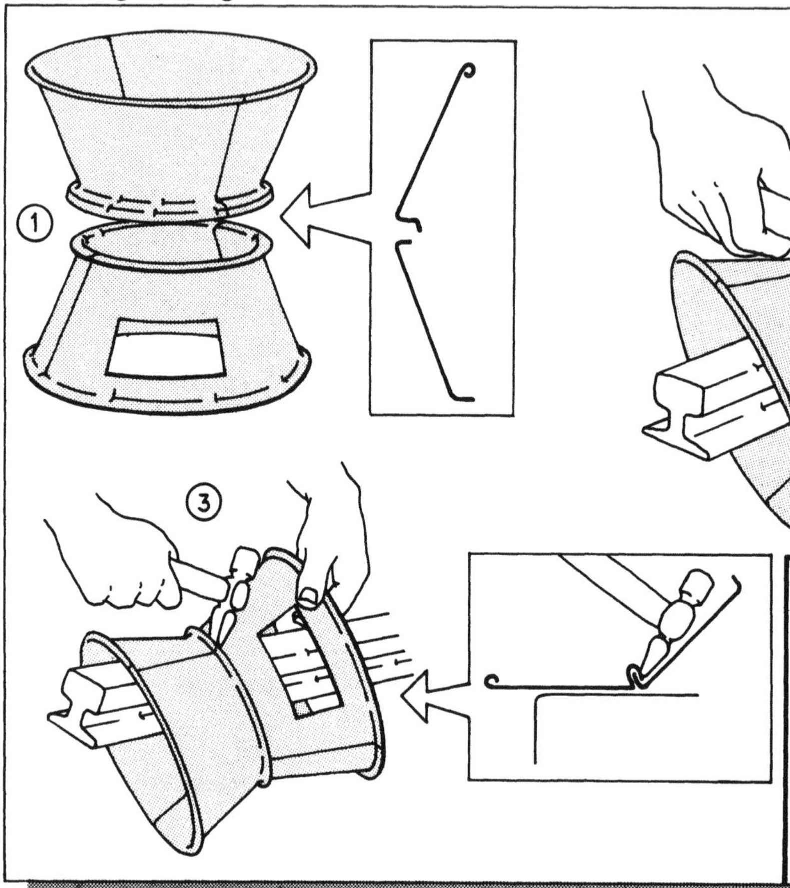

(1) Upper & lower halves placed together.
(2) Initial bending
(3) Final joining

Figure 4.8

Airgate

Now that the basic casing has been made, the stove-maker works on the parts that have to be attached. These consist of the airgate, pot-rests, carrying handles and base.

Using templates 2, 5, 6 and 7 (Figure 4.3) the airgate and hinge parts are cut out, as are the parts needed for the latch. The metal needed to make the hinge (Figure 4.9(3) is cut using the template reserved for the pot-rest holders and feet (Figure 4.3(7)).

It is not necessary to use heavy material for the airgate. The recommended thickness is 0.25–0.5mm, since the airgate only serves a useful purpose if it fits closely and restricts the flow of air to the bottom of the grate. If very stiff material is used, folds and bends in the gate are likely to leave openings that allow air to enter below the grate. If the material is thin, and curved to a larger radius than the casing, when the airgate is closed it will rest against the casing under pressure. Therefore, it will provide a

Airgate

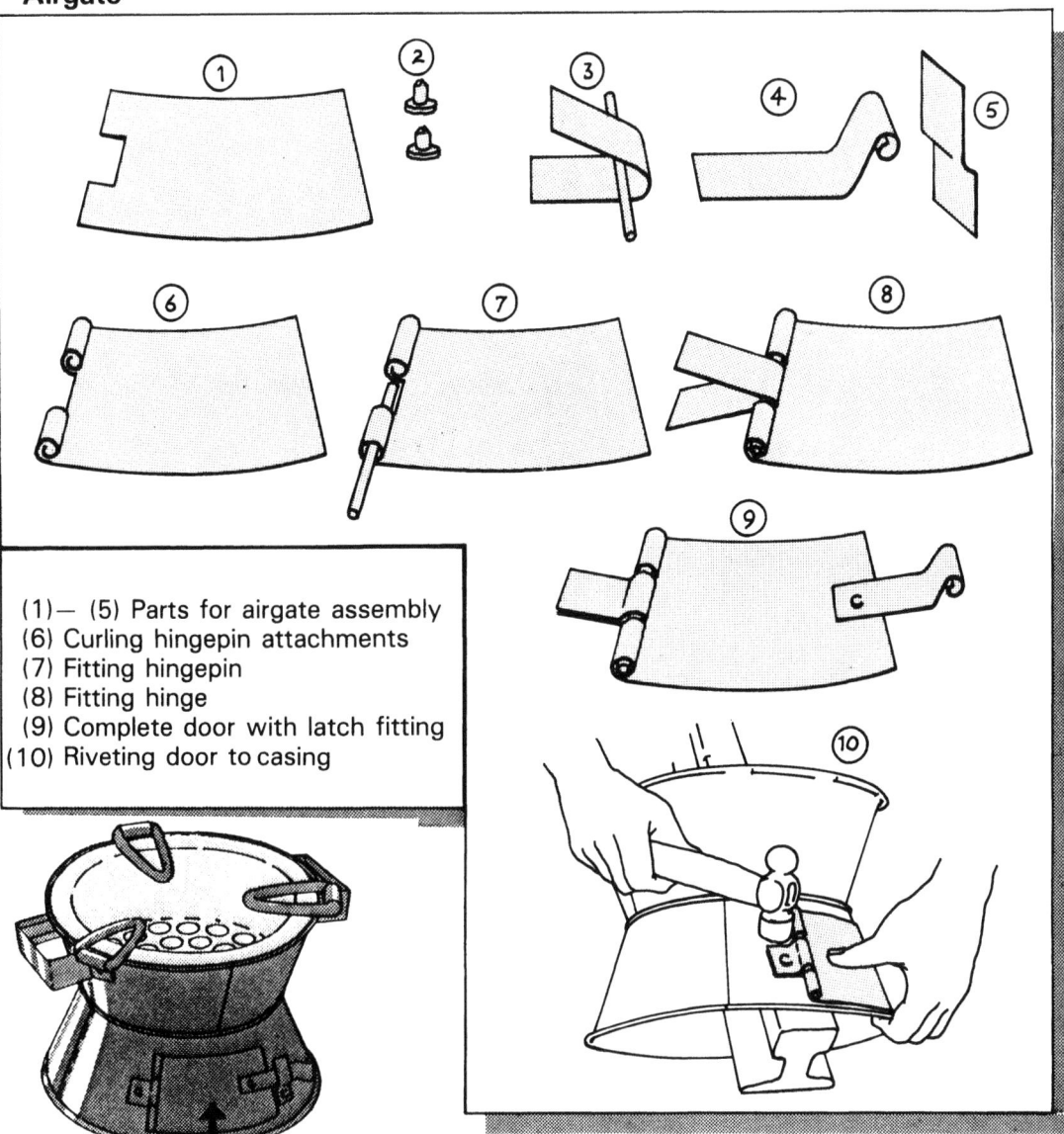

(1)– (5) Parts for airgate assembly
(6) Curling hingepin attachments
(7) Fitting hingepin
(8) Fitting hinge
(9) Complete door with latch fitting
(10) Riveting door to casing

Figure 4.9

better seal against the entry of air. A certain springiness in the gate helps in this respect, and this is more easily achieved by using a thinner sheet.

The hinge should be made from thicker material, since it is attached to the casing by a single rivet. Use of a second rivet is appropriate, but rarely done.

Pot-rest Holders

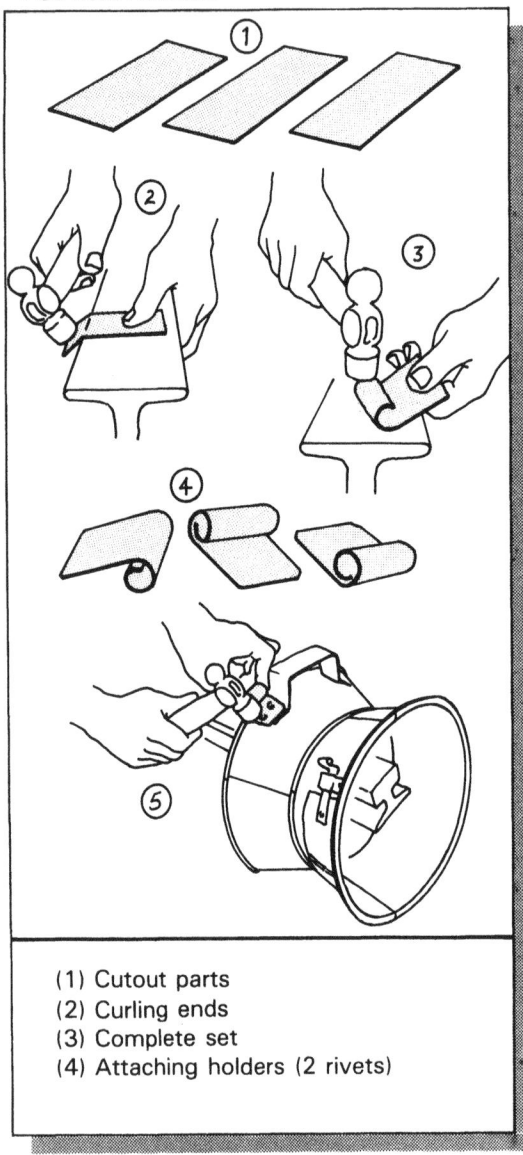

(1) Cutout parts
(2) Curling ends
(3) Complete set
(4) Attaching holders (2 rivets)

Figure 4.10

Pot-rest holders

The pot-rest holders are made from thicker sheet steel than any other part of the stove: 0.8–1.0mm. The pot-rests are hinged from the holders, and rest on the folded lip of the upper half-casing. When a pot is put on the rests it transmits a powerful leverage force to the holder, tending to uncurl the folds as can be seen in Figure 4.10(4).

The holders must be riveted to the casing with two rivets. If a single rivet is used, the holder will loosen and fall off. When this happens, the pot must be placed directly on the charcoal, which means that much of the potential efficiency of the stove is lost.

In Figure 4.10(5), the pot-rest holder is shown held on with two rivets, which are drilled through both the casing and the carrying handle. This is done to reduce the number of rivets needed and to reinforce the pot-rest attachment. Figure 4.10(5) shows that two of the three pot-rest holders share a rivet with the carrying handle.

If thin casing material is being used, and if cooking pots are heavy, it is a good idea to cut a small square of metal and reinforce the casing as shown in Figure 4.11.

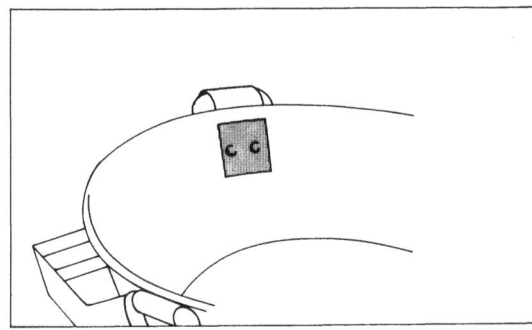

Figure 4.11: *Pot-rest holder reinforcement*

Pot-rests

The pot-rests are made from mild steel roundbar at least 8mm in diameter (see Figure 4.12). Attempts have been made to use 6mm or even thinner materials for the pot-rests. A thicker roundbar has proven more desirable because the rests are exposed to higher heat than any other metal part of the stove. Therefore, they rust very quickly. Material 6mm in diameter will only last half as long as 8mm bar. In addition, heavy pots will bend a thin pot-rest, especially when it gets hot and slightly

Pot-rests

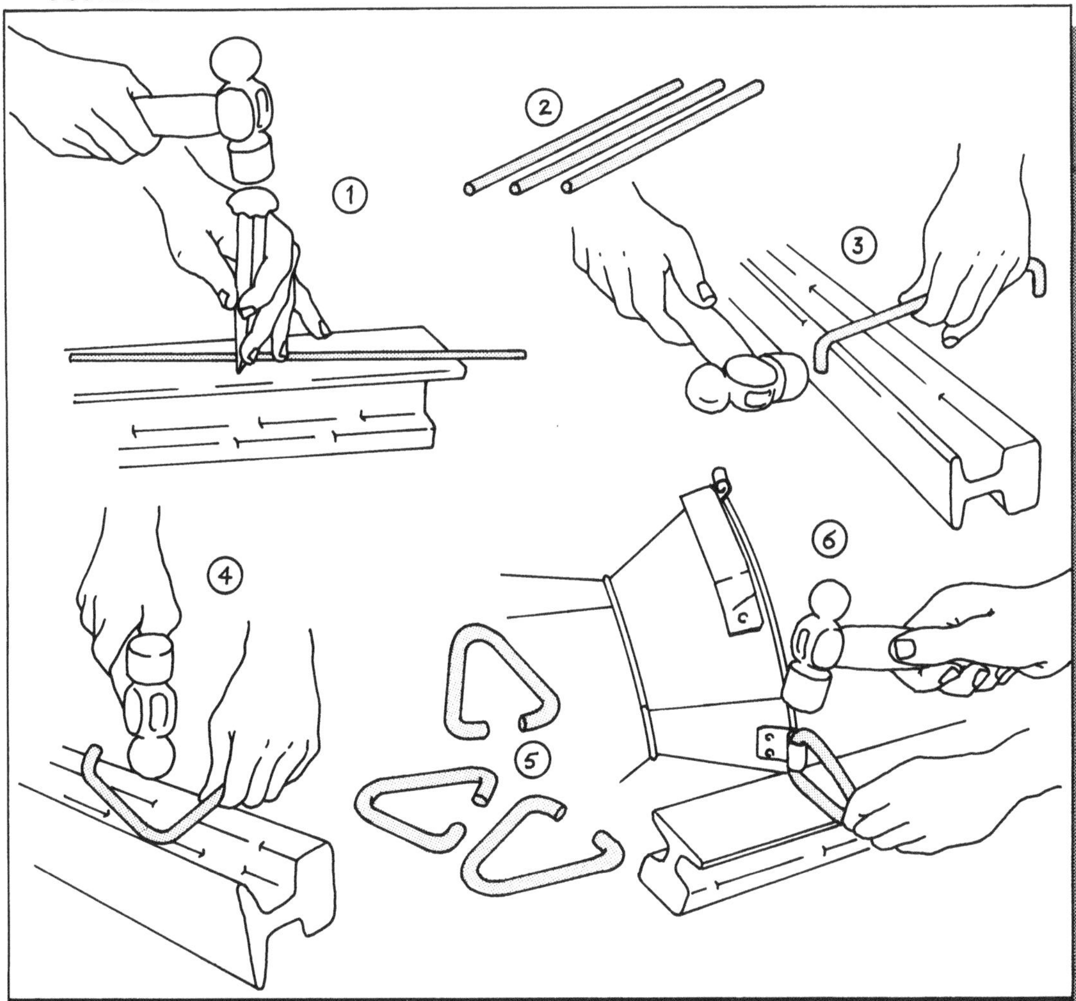

(1) Cutting material
(2) Cutout parts
(3) First bends
(4) Second bends
(5) Complete set
(6) Attaching potrests

Figure 4.12

malleable. In Kenya, Rwanda, Sudan and Uganda, 8mm material (0.3") is the standard.

Pot-rests should be positioned accurately. They should be 120° from each other around the circumference of the stove. It is worth making a simple fixture to enable the stove-maker to position the pot-rests accurately every time. Stove users inform us that equal positioning of the pot-rests is one of the most important characteristics they look for, because if the rests are even slightly irregular, the pot will not be stable when placed carelessly on the stove. Standard dimensions are given in Figure 4.13.

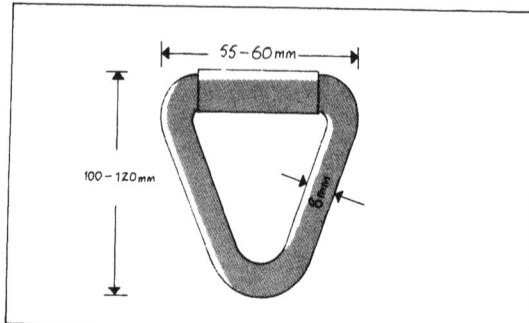

Figure 4.13: *Pot-rest dimensions*

Carrying handles

The carrying handles must be made with care because the stove is often carried from one place to another filled with hot coals and loaded with boiling liquids and hot food. Although this practice is not recommended, people will do it anyway. The stove must be engineered to withstand the loads imposed under these circumstances. The main strut of the handle must be far enough away from the casing to avoid the risk of burning, and close enough to minimize mechanical loads.

The standard dimensions for the handle are given; these apply to all three sizes of stove.

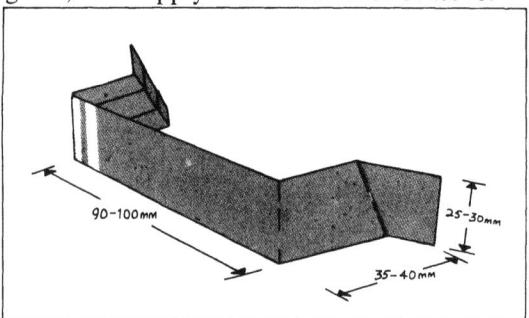

Figure 4.14: *Handle dimensions*

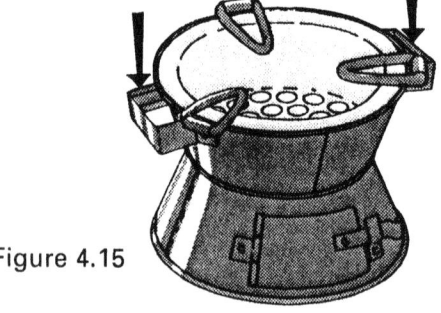

Figure 4.15

Carrying Handles

(1) Cutout parts
(2) & (3) First folds
(4) & (5) Second folds
(6) & (7) Third folds
(8) Attaching handles with rivets

Figure 4.15(2) and (3) show the handle being folded along its length. This adds strength and rigidity and makes it more comfortable to carry the stove. (8) shows the handle being attached to the stove before riveting the pot-rest holders but this is usually done at the same time.

Base

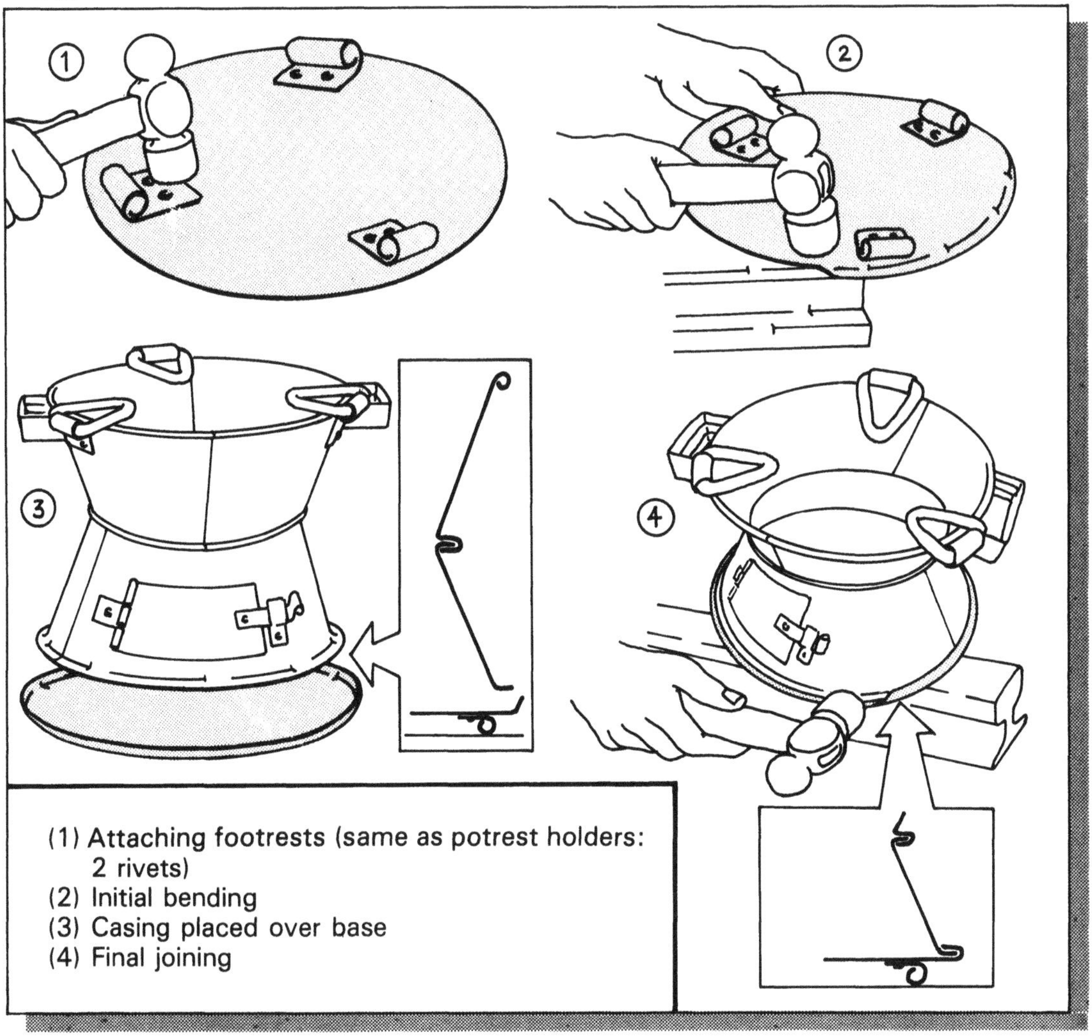

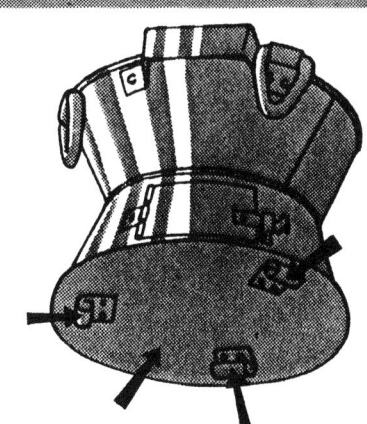

(1) Attaching footrests (same as potrest holders: 2 rivets)
(2) Initial bending
(3) Casing placed over base
(4) Final joining

Figure 4.16

Although this drawing shows a single rivet being used to attach the handle, two rivets are recommended to give extra strength and security.

Base

The base of the stove is made from thin sheet metal, 0.25–0.5mm thick. The base bears no mechanical loads and is protected from heat by a layer of insulation material.

A template is not needed for this part, which is usually marked out by using a pair of metal compasses set to scribe the correct diameter. This diameter is about 10mm greater than the outer diameter of the flange of the lower half-casing.

After the base is cut, the foot-rests are attached, as close to the edge of the stove as possible, but not so close as to interfere with the folded joint. The closer the foot-rests are to the edge of the stove the more stable, and safer, the stove will be. Figure 4.17 gives typical spacing dimensions. Foot-rests should be spaced equally at 120° angles if the stove is to be safe. A simple marking fixture should be used to do this.

The foot-rests are attached using two rivets, to ensure that one or more of the rests will not swing out of place and make the stove unstable.

Once the feet have been attached the circumference of the base is curled up as shown in Figure 4.16(2) and the profile accompanying Figure 4.16(3).

Figure 4.16(4) shows how the base is initially folded over the flange on the lower casing-half. To ensure a tight seal, the joint is finished by beating from above with the engineer's hammer.

Preparation of cementitious material and assembly of liner to casing

The ceramic liner must be made to an accurate size, so that it will be neither tight nor loose in the casing. Because it is difficult to make either the casing or the liner to very high standards of accuracy, the fit between the stove and the liner is sized so that there is a difference of about 15mm between the external diameter of the casing and the external diameter of the liner. The gap is filled with cement, which also attaches the liner to the casing. The difference in diameter ensures that the liner can be pressed about 3–5mm below the rim of the casing, and still allow enough space for the cement filler.

Properly formulated cement, mixed and cured for a sufficient time, firmly bonds the casing and the liner together. There is no need for any other form of direct attachment. Because the cement is protected from direct exposure to the burning charcoal, it retains its strength indefinitely.

The bonding mixture used in Kenya consists of 1 part cement to 4 parts of fine vermiculite dust, which is easily obtained in Nairobi. This is a good mixture because the vermiculite is an insulator and improves the performance of the stove.

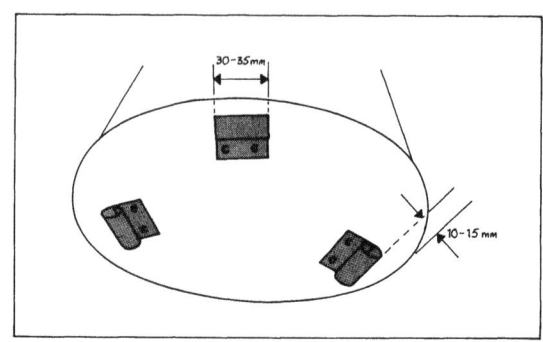

Figure 4.17: *Positioning of the foot-rests on the finished stove*

In many countries vermiculite is not available. Figure 4.18(1) shows the mixtures used in different countries of East Africa. It is important to experiment with various mixtures to see if the liner remains firmly bonded to the casing for several weeks, even when, contrary to recommendations, the stove is turned upside down and shaken, as is often done in cleaning.

The cement mixture is used not only to bond the liner to the casing but to cover the floor with an insulating layer. The mixture is 6–10mm thick and is poured into the open casing before the liner is put in (Figure 4.18(2)). If the airgate hole is properly cut into the casing there will be a lip of about this depth from the bottom of the airgate to the base of the stove. When the insulating cement mixture is put into the stove it is poured to this level.

Assembly of liner to casing

The strength of the bond between the liner and the casing depends on how carefully this work is done, and the patience and integrity of the stove-maker. Cement gains in strength as it cures *if the drying process is slow*. Cements applied to a dry liner will quickly deteriorate, causing the liner to come loose and fall out of the casing.

Before assembly the pottery liner should be soaked in a bucket of water until air bubbles stop coming out of it. This may take 5 minutes. The liner is then allowed to drain for another 5 minutes until no wetness can be seen on the surface.

At this point the liner is ready to be cemented into place.

Preparation of cementitious material in base of casting

(1) Material used and quantity as in Kenya, Rwanda and Sudan.
(2) Put mixture in the casing floor
(3) Cross-section showing casing floor.

If one hour passes, and the liner has not been cemented into place, it should be re-soaked.

When the liner is properly damp, it should be evenly coated with an appropriate cement mixture to a depth of about 6–10mm. This is shown in Figure 4.19(1).

The liner is then firmly pressed into the casing. Do not bang it into position. If the liner does not fit properly in the casing, there is too much cement on the liner. Remove the liner from the casing and scrape off some of the cement. When it is properly set in the casing the rim of the liner should be seated 3–5mm below the metal lip. When the liner is fixed in the casing, liquid cement is dripped into any cavities still showing between the liner and the casing and then smoothed with a spatula (Figure 4.19(3) and (4)).

After the damp liner is cemented into the casing, as shown, the stove should not be sold for at least one week.

Figure 4.18

Because the liner will still be damp, it could crack if heated with charcoal. The dampness ensures that the cement mixture cures slowly, to gain maximum strength. Storing stoves for a week until they cure may be troublesome but this practice ensures a durable product and results in satisfied customers.

After a week, the stove can be painted. Although painting is not necessary, the KCJ usually is painted black. Painting gives the stove a modern look and hides the unsightly cement joint between the casing and the liner.

Assembly of Liner to Casing

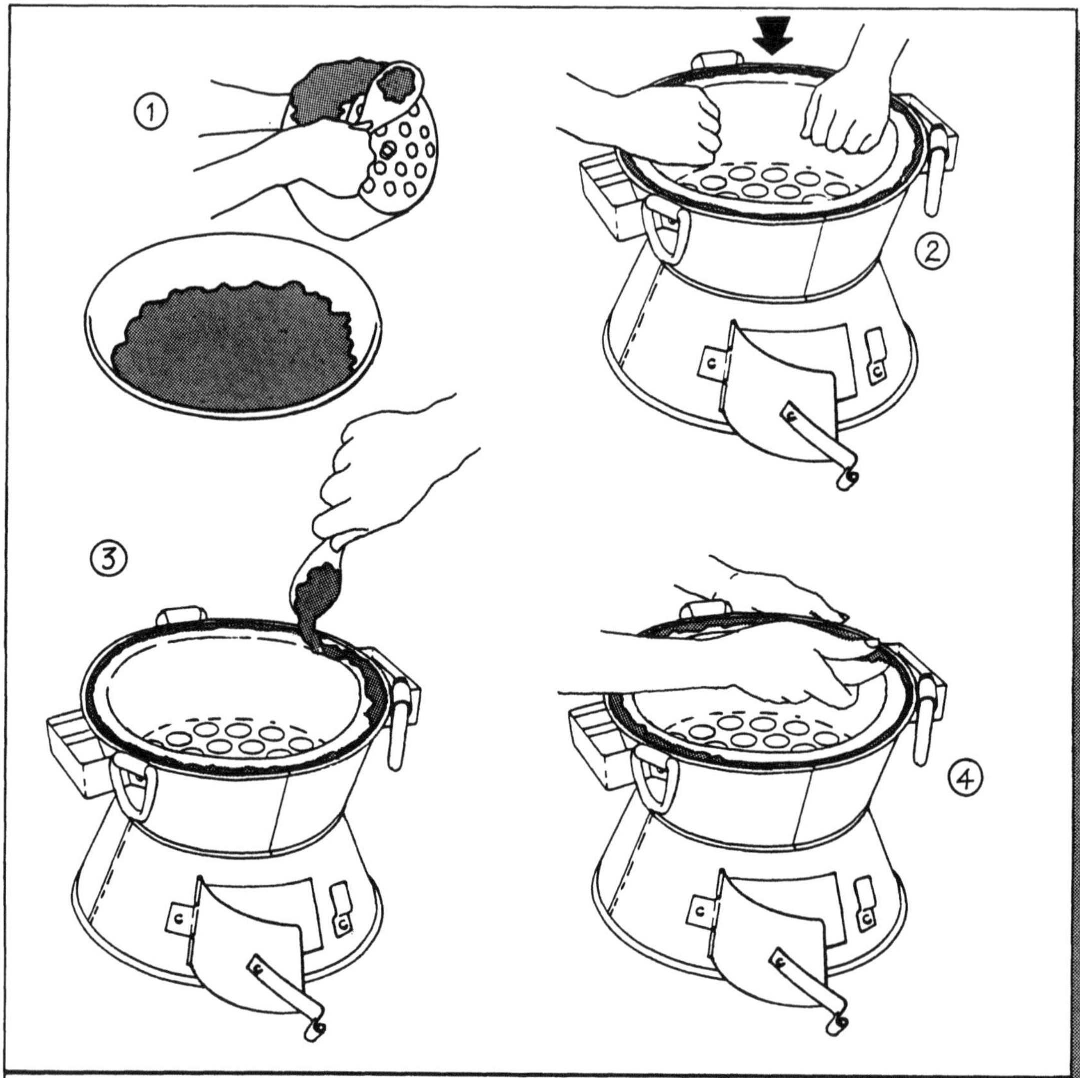

(1) Coating the liner with mixture
(2) Pressing liner into casing
(3) Filling minor gaps between liner and casing with mixture.
(4) Smoothing the surface with a spatula or knife.

Figure 4.19

CHAPTER 5

Ceramic research

The KCJ can be distinguished from other types of fuel efficient charcoal-burning stoves because it uses a ceramic liner, and it blends sheet metal and ceramic technologies. Some people assume that making the ceramic liner is simply a matter of introducing a new product to a competent local potter or to a womens' group. They overlook the fact that the technology involved is fairly sophisticated and that it may take as much as 3–12 months to find a clay, finalize the clay body (clay and other materials mixed) and verify the strength of the finished product.

This chapter contains practical suggestions for finding, developing and testing clays and clay bodies. We want to emphasize the fact that these are practical suggestions based on the author's experience in the field and adapted to the limited resources available in most field settings. If a would-be entrepreneur needs additional help, she or he may want to consult a local ceramic expert. The expert, not necessarily an engineer, would most likely be found at a large-scale brickworks in the country, a large-scale commercial pottery or a minerals-holding company, and ideally will have worked on production of refractory ceramics, especially firebricks, and will be familiar with locally available materials and how they interact when mixed.

Finding clay

A ceramic liner needs to have:

o physical strength;
o ability to resist thermal (heat) shock; and
o insulating capability.

The best type of clay to use in liner making has the following characteristics (in order of priority):

o good physical strength when fired to 900°C (similar to the strength of a good quality flowerpot);
o remains slightly porous when fired to 1150°C increasing in weight by more than 10 per cent when soaked in water;
o does not warp when fired to 1250°C;
o fires to a light salmon colour, between pink and white;
o shrinks less than 8 per cent from a plastic state to dry; and
o plasticity.

The first two characteristics are the most important because they describe the material quality of the finished liner. The last four characteristics are only guides to finding the right sort of clay. In other words, if a clay shrinks less than 8 per cent and fires to a light colour, it is likely to dry without cracking, retain porosity at high temperatures, retain its shape and have good physical strength. If it is plastic, it is a secondary clay and will have a better fired strength than a primary clay such as kaolin (china clay). (For a discussion of primary and secondary clays, see pp. 6–7.)

These guidelines should also be interpreted with caution. For example, it is possible to find red clays that make good liners, as was the case in Sudan. Nevertheless, because most red clays will be difficult to formulate into a good liner body, lighter coloured alternatives, if available, should be tried first.

A similar caveat applies to shrinkage. The Sudanese red clay shrinks as much as 15 per cent from wet to dry, but still makes a good liner. Nevertheless, although it was finally formed into an acceptable body, it caused more problems than CARE encountered in any other country where it introduced the KCJ. (Lighter burning, low-shrinkage clays were available in those countries.)

The most practical way to find a good clay is to look at clays from sites where traditional pottery has been made. This clay may be suitable for making a KCJ liner because, in many parts of the world, traditional clay pots are placed directly over a flame and resist thermal shock. Traditional potters (usually women well known in particular regions for the quality of their pots) will know what clays are available locally. They, or their relatives, may also be able to provide information on the processing steps (crushing, or adding of other ingredients) needed to prepare the local clay for pot-making. Check to make sure that the potters' products are strong (or as strong as possible with traditional firing) and, if possible, fired to a light colour.

In Sudan, Rwanda and Kenya, CARE was able to locate a suitable clay for liner-making by investigating traditional sources of clay. If this does not yield results, geological surveys may be helpful, provided that they are available and that a local expert can help interpret them. If it is necessary to prospect for a previously unused or undiscovered clay, a general rule of thumb is that the most extensive and consistent deposits of plastic clay are *not* usually found at the bottoms of valleys. Often these valley-floor deposits are quite varied and limited. It is better to look for clays in wide flood plains where the flow of water is slower and more gentle.

Look for a flat flood plain (as small as a few hundred metres in extent) in hill areas. Clays found in these places are likely to be fine, plastic, well sorted and relatively uncontaminated since they will have travelled only a short distance from their primary source (clays which have been transported a long way have often picked up a lot of silt, sand, iron and organic contamination).

If the area in question tends to flood at the time of any annual rains, or at least is known for being soft and boggy, this is a promising sign that clay can be found there. Often these places are not farmed because they are too damp, and are used only for seasonal grazing as common land. Grasses growing there will tend to be coarse and tufted.

Unfortunately, clays located within a few kilometres of each other, which seem similar at first glance, may prove very different when tested. Because clays are so varied, and it is so difficult to predict how they will react to firing, it is a good idea to select at least 10 samples for testing. Even if the clays are not suitable to use separately, they may turn out to be serviceable when combined. In Kenya and Uganda, KCJ liners are made from a single clay. In many other countries where it was not possible to find the perfect clay, the liners are made from a mixture of two clays, as well as other materials.

At this point, we are confining our discussion to selecting a clay that would be worth considering as an ingredient in a liner body. How one develops a good clay body is described on pp. 35–7.

Testing the clay

This preliminary testing process is to determine if the clay is suitable and worth considering as an ingredient in a liner body. It is not the same as testing a clay body. Although these are practical tests and not laboratory exercises, it is strongly recommended that you use a consistent system of measurement and a detailed system of record-keeping. Selection of clays to be tested should be based on the following preliminary criteria: convenience of the site, ease of extraction and plasticity.

The necessary equipment consists of:

○ scales, capable of accurately measuring 1kg in 1g increments;
○ mortar and pestle;
○ steel rule, 30cm long in 1mm increments;
○ measuring cylinder, 500cc capacity;
○ bucket;
○ 3mm mesh sieve;
○ wooden frame with ejector, open top and bottom measuring internally 130 × 50 × 25mm; and
○ electric test kiln able to fire up to 1000°C, equipped with a thermocouple and pyrometer able to measure accurately by 10° increments. Colleges, potteries and industrial research organizations have electric test kilns and are usually happy to help in the testing process. Engineering companies that harden metal will have similar equipment.

There are four basic properties to be tested:

○ clay content
○ shrinkage
○ water absorption
○ fired strength

Clay content: Most clays are mixed with sand, gravel, silts and other minerals. Discovering how much of the material collected is in fact clay is important. If there are too many non-clay materials it will be too expensive to purify a clay into a usable body. Some elements, even in small quantities (lime is a particular culprit) will make even the best clays useless.

To test the clay content, thoroughly dry 1kg of clay, then break it into powder in the mortar and pestle. Pound only long and hard enough to break up the clay; do not attempt to crush the small stones and sand that separate themselves from the clay during this process.

When all the clay is thoroughly broken up, it is dry mixed on a flat board with a trowel to make sure that all the particles of every type are evenly distributed. When this is done measure 200g very carefully on the scales and mix this material with 300g of water until the particles have dissolved. Shake the clay and water vigorously in a bottle until it forms a thin cream (slip). Pass the slip through the sieve, put into the glass measuring-cylinder and allow to settle for two days. The stones and grit left behind on the screen must be carefully measured by volume in the measuring-cylinder.

After two days, the clay and other materials will have settled to the bottom of the measuring-cylinder. There will be a layer of clear water on top. Pour off the water. Looking through the walls of the cylinder it will be possible to see the larger grits and sands at the bottom of the cylinder, and the finer clays at the top.

If there appears to be more than 40 per cent sand and gravel in the clay, by volume, then the clay is probably not suitable for liner-making. It would be very expensive to refine large amounts of this clay for this purpose. If the proportion of the visible grit in the measuring-cylinder when added to the material rejected by the sieve exceeds 50 per cent, it is again unwise to make use of the clay, unless you are prepared to pay high refining costs.

This simple test indicates whether the level of sand and gravel in the clay is acceptable. Even though the coarser sands can help a clay resist thermal shock, reduce drying shrinkage and prevent cracks in drying, too much sand and too many large particles will weaken a fired body.

Shrinkage: All clays shrink, but the degree of shrinkage varies. A clay that shrinks more than 10 per cent is difficult to work with because it will tend to warp and crack as it dries, unless exceptional care is taken to control and slow down the natural drying process.

Cracks occur because the clay on the outside of the newly formed piece dries before the clay on the inside, tending to contract and squeeze the floor of the liner. Once the walls become dry and rigid, the base will start to shrink; because the base is attached to the walls it will tend to separate and crack.

Sometimes these cracks are barely visible, and only show up when the liner is in use. More often they develop while the liner dries. Standard liners made in Kenya from a clay that shrank 12 per cent had cracking rates in drying of 32 per cent until drying was artificially slowed down by placing liners in a cool, moist room. Even then the rate was still 10 per cent. The best clays, which are still plastic, have shrinkage rates of 5–8 per cent.

To test for shrinkage, the dry clay remaining from the clay-content tests is sieved through the 3mm screen and mixed with 30 per cent water by weight into a thoroughly plastic condition. It is then pressed firmly into a wooden frame which measures (internally) 130 × 50 × 25mm. Before the clay is pressed inside, the wooden frame is dampened and lightly dusted with wood-ash to ensure that the clay will be released easily. The clay blank is pushed out of the frame using the fitted wooden ejector and set to dry on a flat wooden surface covered with canvas.

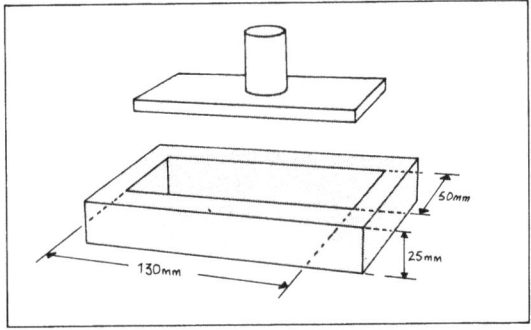

Figure 5.1: *Wooden frame and ejector for making test blanks*

A thin line is lightly drawn along the centre axis of the clay, and marked very carefully with crossbars set exactly 100mm apart. The blank should be turned over every hour or two to ensure that it dries evenly on both sides.

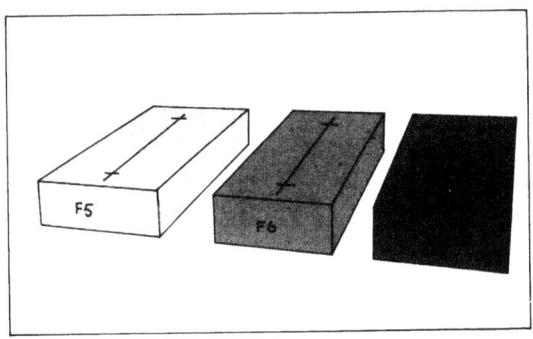

Figure 5.2: *Test blanks with crossbar markings to measure shrinkage*

At least five such samples should be made for each type of clay being tested. This will not only provide a good range of samples but will allow other tests (water absorption and strength) to be conducted from the same batch.

After the clay is completely dried and placed in direct sunlight for at least two additional hours, the amount of shrinkage should be measured, together with any other noticeable changes such as cracking or warping. This is easily done by comparing the distance between the crossbars before and after drying. Before drying all the crossbars will be 100mm apart. If after drying a particular sample has decreased in length to 88mm, it has shrunk 12 per cent.

All five samples should be measured this way to estimate the average shrinkage. At this stage, clays with shrinkage greater than 12 per cent should be avoided if at all possible, while a clay with less than 10 per cent shrinkage is promising. A clay with a shrinkage lower than 8 per cent has high potential, especially if kaolin (china clay) is available as an additive.

A clay will shrink further when it is fired, although usually no more than an additional 1 per cent. Nevertheless, a note should be made of the total shrinkage from a wet to a fired condition, after the blank is fired to 900°C. This will help when it comes to designing production tooling for the moulding machinery (jigger-jolley — see p. 49.).

Water absorption: Porosity in a ceramic liner is important for two reasons: it improves the insulating qualities of a particular clay; and it helps the clay withstand thermal shock when it is unevenly and rapidly heated and cooled. A clay that is hard-fired and no longer porous will be quite strong physically but will crack very quickly when used, because its very density makes it too rigid to withstand sudden heating and cooling.

On the other hand, a clay liner that is too porous will tend to be too weak to withstand the physical punishment imposed by cooking. A water absorption rate of between 15–22 per cent is an acceptable range for a ceramic liner.

To test for water absorption the fired clay blanks are heated to over 100°C and carefully weighed. They are then dropped in water and boiled for approximately half an hour. The water is allowed to cool and the blanks taken out and rolled on a dry cloth to remove surface moisture. They are then weighed once more. The increase in weight is divided by the original weight and multiplied by 100 to give the percentage of water absorption.

For example, if the clay blank weighed 211g before soaking and 247g after soaking the percentage of absorption can be calculated as follows:

Original weight of blank	211
Weight of wet blank	247
Increase in weight	36

$(36/211) \times 100$ 17.06% water absorption

The water absorption test can indicate whether too much lime is present. If so, the fired clay blanks will break up and disintegrate into coarse powder, despite having considerable dry strength. This occurs because lime, when wetted in the clay, rehydrates after firing. A clay that is fired to 900°C but cracks or crumbles when soaked must be rejected.

Fired strength: There are standard laboratory tests to determine fired strength, but most liner-makers do not have access to a laboratory. It is important to know which of the clays are strongest and which are weakest. A practical alternative to determine the fired tensile strength of various fired clays is the following:

○ Rest dried test bars which have been fired to 900°C on two triangular supports, placed 100mm apart.
○ A bucket of known weight is suspended by a wire from the centre of the test bar. A known quantity of water is slowly poured into the bucket until sufficient weight is added to break the bar. The quantity of water added is noted.
○ The weight of the bucket plus the water added to the bucket is a measure of the tensile strength of each bar.
○ The test should be repeated at least three times on bars from each clay sample to obtain a more representative average.

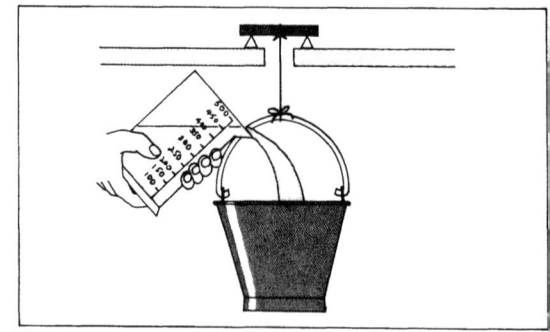

Figure 5.3: *Testing to compare fired strength of different samples*

It is important that the bars come from the same clay batch, are formed in the same wooden frame, fired to the same temperature and dried to the same level (completely dry) before testing.

Interpreting the results

An ideal clay will have a low shrinkage rate (below 8 per cent), a water-absorption percentage of 15–22 per cent, and a high strength in comparison to other samples. A clay with a high shrinkage rate, water-absorption percentage outside the recommended limits and comparative weakness is not suitable.

In practice most clays will have some good characteristics, and some less desirable ones. The main criteria for selecting clay for further testing and development are:

○ relatively good strength
○ low shrinkage
○ optimal percentage of water absorption

Having rank-ordered the clays being tested, it is a good idea to make liners from the best three samples, to see if the clay in its natural state is a good material for liners. If such a clay can be identified, it eliminates the need for strict supervision and control over the mixing process.

To test the clays, make 20 liners from each type of clay, and fire them to between 850–900°C. If the drying is carefully controlled and four or more of the liners crack in formation and drying, the clay is unsuitable without further development. Five of the liners from each batch of clay should then be heated in a charcoal forge to an orange-red colour and immediately plunged into a bucket of cold water. The liners should then be inspected for cracks. If there are no cracks, the liners should be allowed to dry thoroughly once again, before they are reheated and the test is repeated. This process, known as an accelerated destruction test, has proven to be a most reliable gauge of a liner's durability and strength.

A clay that is suitable for liner-making would have no visible cracks in any of the samples manufactured, nor after heating and quenching twice. Liners from batches that pass all these tests should be fitted into stove casings, and given to users for actual field testing. The users selected should be people who cook intensively all day, such as tea sellers and restaurant owners, and who are near the testing centre.[1]

Each week, someone should check to determine if the stoves are using fuel efficiently and if they remain free of serious cracks. After three months, when the tests have been concluded, it is advisable still to check the condition of the liners each month. It is very unlikely, however, that a single clay in an unmodified form will be good enough for liner-making. This is why only a few samples are made for firing and field testing. Below we suggest methods and materials for developing a good clay mixture.

Developing a good clay mixture (body)

There are hundreds of materials that can be added to make a better liner body. Ideally even after a clay body has been developed, research should be continuous to make sure that the liner remains efficient and durable. In practice, only a limited number of additive materials is easily available and affordable. These fall into three basic categories: other clays; organic openers; and sands.

Other clays: A clay may be ideal for liner-making but insufficiently plastic to form on a moulding machine. The addition of a small amount of a more plastic clay or bentonite, (as little as 2 per cent) can make the necessary difference. On the other hand, a plastic clay may be too dense, producing a liner that is brittle and prone to cracking in use. Adding sawdust and china clay to a plastic clay will increase the maturing temperature of the main clay, and reduce both its rates of shrinkage and plasticity. (Maturing temperature is the temperature at which the clay acquires the permanent characteristics which suit its intended use.)

Descriptive records should be kept not only of such qualities as shrinkage and water absorption but also of plasticity and estimated refractory quality (its ability to withstand high temperatures). This record should be kept not only for clays which are considered to have potential as liner-making material but also the clays which are *not* suitable, because they may still contribute useful properties to a mixture.

Table 5.1 indicates the common characteristics of the main groups of clays, and their contribution to the behaviour of a body.

Even small percentage changes in the

---

1. An excellent methodology for testing the performance of stoves, both from a laboratory and a user's point of view, is suggested by Bill Stewart in his book, *Improved Wood, Waste and Charcoal Burning Stoves*, IT Publications, 1987.

Table 5.1: *Clays and their common characteristics*

Clay Type	Characteristics
Red clays (marls and brick-earths)	Positive: Generally contribute plasticity to a clay body Reduce maturing temperature of a body if the other materials are fireclays or kaolins Add bonding strength to more refractory clays
	Negative: Tend to be contaminated with silt, organic matter and soil Generally increase shrinkage If used alone, tend to be too dense and brittle
Kaolins (China clays)	Positive: Reduce overall shrinkage Increase maturing temperature of the body Lighten the body colour
	Negative: Reduce mechanical strength, which is extremely poor if used alone Have very poor plasticity
Fireclays and ballclays	Positive: Have good plasticity Have excellent strength Excellent refractory quality Ideal density
Bentonites	Positive: In small proportions (a maximum of 5 per cent) contribute plasticity
	Negative: Extremely high shrinkage rate; cannot be used alone or in high proportions

mixture of various clays in a body may result in significant changes in the body's usefulness for making liners. This is why it is important to test several mixtures of varying proportions and to try and discern general trends in performance which relate to changes in the proportions of materials used. This will prove valuable in the future, particularly if the quality of the main clay reserve begins to vary. Understanding how each material contributes to the overall quality and performance of the liner is important if the manufacturer is to be self-sufficient.

Organic openers: Adding certain organic compounds, such as sawdust and rice-husk ash, to clay can be beneficial: they promote even drying, reduce shrinkage and can add a fuel which is burned during firing. On the minus side they reduce the plasticity of the clay and, in excessive quantity, can cause cracking when fired. Generally they do not weaken the body as does sand. A clay with 20 per cent fine sawdust or rice-husk ash present by volume is usually much stronger than the same clay with an addition of 20 per cent sand.

A clay mixed with some sawdust can make a far better liner because:

○ Sawdust converts the clay matrix into a fine honeycomb of very small air voids. This improves the insulating properties of the liners.
○ The small air voids open up the body and give it a very slight flexibility. This helps the clay to better resist thermal shock.

Together with rice-husk ash, sawdust is probably the best organic opener, but care must be taken to use only fine material, preferably from a sawmill rather than a carpenter's workshop where sawdust is usually mixed with wood shavings. Fine hardwood sawdust from a circular saw will be ideal for liner-making. Sawdust is naturally porous and allows moisture deep inside a body to escape more easily. The most commonly used organic openers in traditional pottery are animal dung (from cows and donkeys) and unburned rice husks.

Our experience in Kenya and Sudan has shown that dungs (particularly donkey dung) have a strong negative effect on the strength of clay bodies. Dung is highly fibrous and limits the ability of the clay to bond. It will help prevent drying cracks, but will weaken the finished product, and is therefore not recommended.

Adding rice husks to a clay will also weaken it if the unmodified husks are used in their natural form. However, if the rice husks are burned to ash and mixed into the clay they promote even drying and help reduce shrinkage. Rice-husk ash can be present up to 15 per cent by weight. Because it contains as much as 90 per cent amorphous silica it helps to reduce the chance of cracking, both in manufacture and use. This makes rice-husk ash particularly valuable in making stove liners. Powdered talc (a mineral) used in amounts of between 5–12 per cent by weight will have a similar effect.

In using organic materials, the best results are obtained when they are passed through a coarse sieve with a mesh dimension of 1.5–2.0mm. Most types of mosquito wire are suitable.

Sands: Sand is present in most secondary clays. It is used as an additive by potters to: reduce shrinkage; promote more even drying; and improve workability by reducing stickiness.

Sand is used to reduce shrinkage, and therefore cracking in drying. The shrinkage rate in clay can be reduced from 10 per cent to as little as 6 per cent if 15–20 per cent sand is added.

There are two essential drawbacks in using sand: a clay with too much sand becomes mechanically weak, and breaks more easily after firing; and sand that is too fine, or has a high percentage of fine particles, contributes to high rates of cracking during firing, particularly during cooling. It is therefore important to use only the minimum necessary to reduce shrinkage and stop cracking in drying. Sand should only be used if organic openers have proved ineffective, cannot be obtained, reduce the workability of the clay below acceptable limits or are already present in the maximum practical amounts.

Different types of sand will yield very different results in a clay. A wide range should be tried because the properties of sand depend on the type of rock from which it is derived. A sand made from crushed granite will have a different effect to sand from a coral beach. Sand derived from granite will be high in feldspar (a plus), while coral sand will be high in calcium (a minus).

Sands obtained from river beds, crushed granite and roadstone are often quite useful, as is silver sand (often called silica sand). *There is no substitute for testing and recording the effects of adding different types and amounts of sands on clay body strength and rates of cracking.*

Sand used in liner-making should be quite coarse, of the quality used by builders, but should be able to pass through a 3–5mm mesh sieve.

Testing methodology

In testing different materials it is important to examine only one factor at a time. If a new clay is added to a mixture together with a different sand, it will not be possible to determine which material has contributed to what changes in the final quality of the body.

Testing should proceed from a study of materials that are likely to be present in the largest proportions, to materials that are likely to be present in small amounts and have minimal effects.

Tables 5.2 and 5.3 are based on actual work done in CARE's stove programme in East Africa. Table 5.2 shows how black and white clays were mixed to arrive at proportions that gave

Table 5.2: *Combined clay test results, all quantities by volume (fired to 900°C)*

Material	Test Number						
	A	B	C	D	E	F	G
Black clay	1	0	3	1	1	2	1
White clay	0	1	1	1	3	1	2
% cracking in drying	12	30	26	24	24	20	28
% cracking in firing	20	26	16	22	24	10	22
% Lost in accelerated destruction tests	30	20	20	20	20	15	20

the best results with respect to cracking in drying, firing and use. Nevertheless, the rates of cracking were still too high to make the body acceptable for use in production.

Table 5.2 shows that best results were obtained from a mixture of 2 parts black clay with 1 part white. With this as a starting point, experiments were conducted with varying additions of sand and sawdust.

Throughout the following tests the ratio of the two different clays was held constant at 2:1, and varying percentages of sand and sawdust were tried. Sand was added in increasing amounts, first 10 per cent, and then 20 per cent, with no other additions to the body. The next two tests excluded sand and used increasing percentages of sawdust, again 10 per cent and 20 per cent.

This meant that the body was tested with a clay content of 100 per cent, 90 per cent and 80 per cent. In addition, a clay content level of 80 per cent was arbitrarily selected, and sawdust and sand added in varying ratios as follows: 1:1, 1:3, 3:1 (tests F5, F6, and F7).

The final body formulation that resulted from the tests shown in Table 5.3 was:

	%	buckets
Black clay	55	11
White clay	25	5
Sand	10	2
Sawdust	15	3

For each batch of tests 50 liners should be made from each clay mixture under conditions identical to those in a production workshop, and on the mechanical moulding equipment. The loss rate is calculated from the declining number of acceptable liners available at each step in the process. For example, a loss of 10 liners in drying is a 20 per cent loss from the original batch of 50, leaving 40 liners available for the next test. Four liners breaking in firing would mean a 10 per cent loss. This would leave 36 for the remaining tests. If 5 liners are then broken (14 per cent), a total of 31 liners would remain from the original batch of 50. The aggregate loss rate in this case would be 38 per cent (19/50 × 100).

Table 5.3: *Body test results, all quantities by volume*

Material	F	F1	F2	F3	F4	F5	F6	F7
Black clay	67	53	60	53	60	53	53	53
White clay	33	27	30	27	30	27	27	27
Sand	0	20	10	0	0	10	15	5
Sawdust	0	0	0	20	10	10	5	15
% cracking in drying	20	6	14	4	8	6	2	4
% cracking in firing	10	10	6	2	8	14	10	6
% lost in accelerated destruction tests	20	20	20	10	10	5	10	0

The results of these tests, as shown in Table 5.3, clearly indicate that adding both sand and sawdust improved the survival rates in all three stages of production, firing and destruction testing.

The best results were obtained when sawdust was used with sand in the ratio of 3:1 (Test F7). Additional tests were conducted with fixed proportions of sand and sawdust, set at 10 per cent and 15 per cent, in which the clay mixtures were once again varied. These additional tests are not included in the tables because there was no improvement in the survival rates and the cracking rate increased when the liner was used in a stove. Cracking was measured after the stove had been used commercially for three months.

Earlier we recommended that only 20 samples be made to test pure clays. Because it is almost certain that a pure clay will be unsuitable without modification, a small batch of 20 liners is sufficient to reveal the gross differences between clays. A larger sample size is needed to test a clay mixture because small differences in material composition may have only a small influence on the performance of the stove. These differences are more likely to be measurable, and their real significance assessed, with a larger test sample. Also, in a larger sample, the differences in firing temperature (in different areas of a production kiln) that can skew the results will tend to even out. Although it is costly to make 50 liners for each type of body to be tested, it should be done to avoid basing important decisions on too small a sample.

Developing a good clay mixture for stove liners is complex and takes time. The initial test of the pure clays will take a relatively short time (1¾ months) as follows:

o prospecting and digging from 10 different clay deposits — 1 month;
o refining, manufacture of test bars, drying and firing — 2 weeks; and
o testing fired bars for shrinkage, porosity and strength — 1 week.

It is likely that at least two series of tests will be needed to develop a final clay mixture. It will be necessary to wait for the results from one series before proceeding with the next.

It probably is not practical to wait for results of user tests (as long as 3 months) before making new mixtures and conducting a second or third series. One way to shorten the testing cycle is to conduct accelerated destruction tests. These have proved a highly reliable guide to the durability and strength of the liner, and are used by CARE and ATI in East Africa. User tests will verify the results of the accelerated destruction tests. (User tests were conducted on batches of 10 stoves; it is too expensive and impractical to keep track of batches of 50 jikos in the field.)

The time required for each series of tests will be 3½ months, as follows:

o preparing 3.5t of clay for making up to 1000 liners, if 20 mixtures are being tested — 3 weeks;
o making and drying 1000 liners — 1½ months;
o firing 1000 liners in two batches — 1 week;
o accelerated destruction tests (5 from each batch) — 1 week (5 weeks in total); and
o fitting perhaps 5 batches of 20 liners to stoves for field testing — 1 week.

A minimum of 2 such series is needed: one to test combinations of clays, and one to test other additives. The initial prospecting and clay-testing takes about 1½ months. If each series of tests takes 3½ months and three such series are needed, it may take almost a year to finalize the clay-body liner. Although it is time-consuming, this research is critical to production of a high quality liner, which is essential for effective stove promotion.

Field tests

We have tried in this section to describe a rigorous method for developing a clay body. If the mixture passes an accelerated destruction test it will almost certainly make good liners. It is useful, however, to realize that clays can behave in quite unpredictable ways. While laboratory tests might indicate serious problems with a body, it is possible that in practice the liners perform very well.

For example, in Togo, over 30 different body mixtures were tested. Although seven of these came through drying and firing without any cracking, not a single liner survived the accelerated destruction tests. It was nevertheless decided to put 70 liners into casings (10 from each series), and field test in Lomé households. To everyone's surprise, (and relief), the liners did not crack, and fuel savings of 40–65 per cent were recorded.

The accelerated destruction tests proved valuable in identifying a mixture that had no tendency to crack across the grate itself, resulting in only narrow fissures in the sidewalls. Putting the liners into casings solved this problem.

We therefore recommend that if cracking cannot be eliminated in accelerated destruction tests, it may still be useful to field test completed stoves made from what seem to be the better mixtures.

Production of the liner

Throwing liners by hand on a potter's wheel is a skill which takes years to develop fully. Yet even a trained thrower cannot match the accuracy and speed of production of an unskilled worker who is using a jigger-jolley.

Using a jigger-jolley confers a decisive advantage over other methods of liner production. Although hand production of liners may be more cost effective when you are testing the market for the KCJ (or if skilled labour is plentiful and inexpensive), mechanized production is generally an important factor in expanding the scale of production and in ensuring liner quality. In reviewing the history of Wambugu's business (see p. 3), it is clear that the jigger-jolley enabled him to produce, and to sell, in a quality-conscious market. For this reason, this manual emphasizes use of this machine, and detailed drawings are available as part of the Engineering Drawing Set (see pp. 75–98). Drawings of the kiln are also provided (pp. 92–98) because a relatively high, even kiln temperature is needed, resulting in far fewer losses and a more durable liner than when an open pit firing is used. A kiln is essential to fire a good quality liner; an open pit is unacceptable for firing this product.

Machinery to crush and mix clay is helpful, but not essential. Although such machines are shown in the manual, engineering drawings are not available as part of this package. The process of manufacturing the liner is shown in a series of drawings similar to those used to illustrate the manufacture of the metal casing. It assumes that research into clays has been completed.[2]

2. For further information on Third World pottery, specifically the use of local clays, the author recommends Henrik Norsker, *The Self-Reliant Potter: Refractories and Kilns*, GATE/GTZ, Eschborn, Germany, 1987.

CHAPTER 6

Producing the liner

Tools for mixing and moulding

The tools in Figure 6.1 are those needed in addition to the moulding and clay-mixing machinery. If clay is prepared by hand, no additional tools are needed except for a heavy wooden crusher, which is not shown. The sieve (1) is made from 5mm galvanized screen material, which is commonly used to screen building sand. A ceramic liner, made by machine, does not require carefully refined clay. Fine clay for tableware is usually passed through extremely fine sieves with gaps of less than 0.25mm. Clay this fine is actually bad for making liners, because it excludes the larger particles and sawdust that help the liner resist heat shock. On the other hand, a screen with a mesh larger than 5mm will allow stones to pass through that will cause the liner to crack as it dries. Any lumps of clay that pass through this mesh are dissolved in the clay preparation process.

Cracks that appear suddenly in a large number of liners, when there has been no change in materials, can nearly always be traced to the sieve, and a single hole which allows larger particles and lumps through. In Wambugu's workshop, as much as 7.5 per cent of the clay is rejected by the screen even after being double crushed. This is a small amount of clay, but if even a little of this material gets past the screen it is surprising how many liners will have to be rejected and reprocessed.

All the other equipment in Figure 6.1 is for general purpose work, except for the bucket (6),

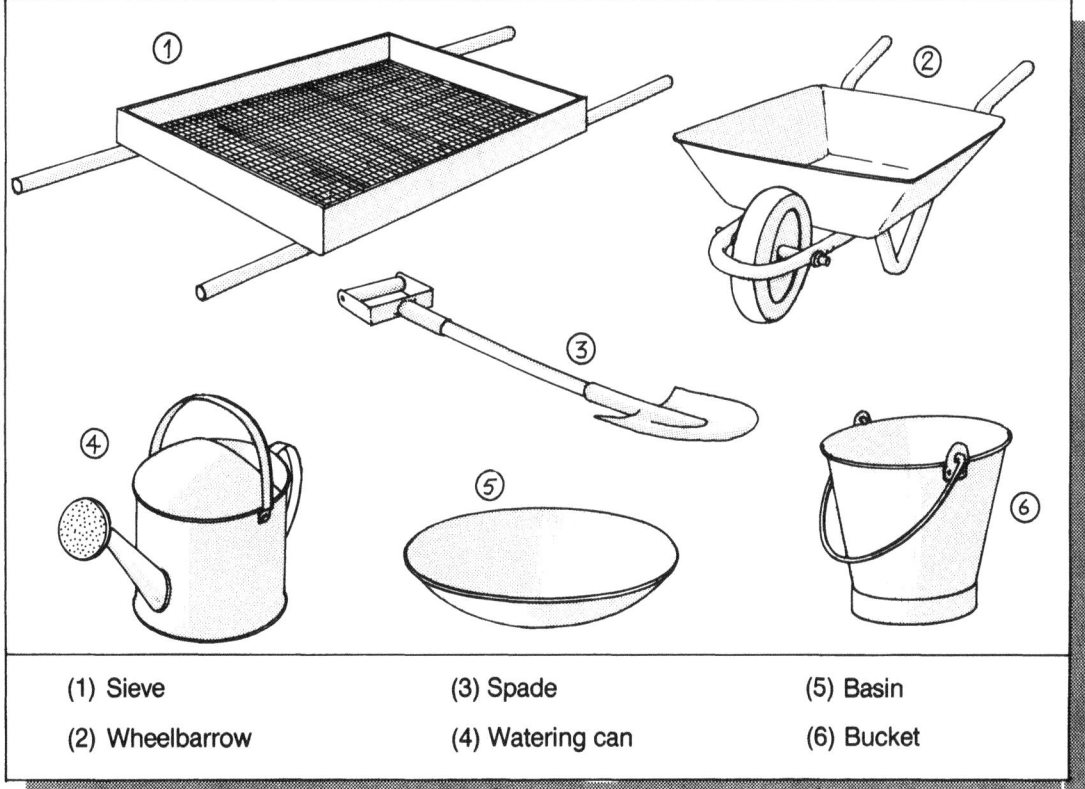

Tools for Mixing and Moulding

(1) Sieve
(2) Wheelbarrow
(3) Spade
(4) Watering can
(5) Basin
(6) Bucket

Figure 6.1

used to measure the ingredients which go into the clay mixture. After the research into clay has yielded a suitable blend of ingredients, this is best explained to the workers in terms of buckets, which should be a standard size. If different-size buckets are used in the workshop, the workers are more likely to make mistakes. On one occasion, Wambugu found that about 5 per cent of his liners were cracking in drying, because a 10-litre bucket had been used to measure the sawdust and a 20-litre bucket to measure sand and clay. The watering can (4) should also be of a standard size, preferably the same volume as the bucket.

Crushing clay manually

The conventional method of preparing clay for making ceramic articles is to break it into small lumps and powder, slake it down with water into a thin liquid (slip), pass this through a fine screen and then, in settling pans, dry out the clay to the correct consistency. This is time-consuming and requires a lot of space, particularly during the rainy seasons when drying takes place very slowly.

Because the clay needed for liners does not have to be so fine, and quite large particles must be allowed into the clay, a dry mixing method is used which eliminates the fine filtration system of the conventional method. This involves crushing the clay, screening the powder and adding just enough water to make the clay plastic and ready for use. No drying pans are needed, and clay can be prepared direct from a dry clay store.

The most important prerequisite is to have enough dry clay to last during wet seasons, when mining clay might be difficult. At Wambugu's factory, enough clay is dug for a minimum of three months' production. Since he produces about 2000 liners a month, he must have enough clay to make 6000 liners. Each liner weighs 3.25kg when wet and 2.65kg dry. Since sand is included in the weight, each liner uses about 2.5kg of dry clay. Thus, he digs about 15t (2 truckloads) of dry clay two weeks before the wet season, which suffices until the clay deposit is accessible again.

Clay can be crushed by hand, using a timber crusher and hammers, as is shown in Figure 6.2. Using this method, it would take two men six hours each to crush enough clay for 200 liners. Harder clays would require more time. Manual clay crushing is an excellent way to produce finely powdered material, but the work is slow and tiring. Finding labourers may be difficult.

Crushing Clay Manually

Crushing dry clay by hand.

Figure 6.2

Crushing clay by machine (Pin mill)

After being in business for over a year Wambugu invested in a locally made clay-crusher which could process material that was too small to crush efficiently by hand — lumps about 1cm in diameter which were discarded after the screening process.

A pin-mill consists of a heavy steel drum containing a heavy (60kg) rotating metal disk, to which are attached two concentric rows of hardened steel pins, 40mm in diameter and about 100mm long (Figure 6.3). In the front of the casing are two further rows of the same pins, but fixed in the casing and set to lie between and inside the rotating pins. A diesel engine of 2.2kW drives the 60kg disk at about 650rpm and dry clay lumps are fed through the entry hole at the centre of the front plate (Figure 6.3:1). The clay has to pass through this series of static and rotating pins, and gets smashed to a powder, 85 per cent of which will pass through a 5mm mesh screen. If the waste material is passed through the mill again about half of the remainder will pass through the screen, making a total of 92–93 per cent that is usable. The material rejected by the screen consists mainly of small stones.

This type of mill is able to process up to 3.5t of clay an hour, although 2.0t is a more normal

Crushing Clay by Machine

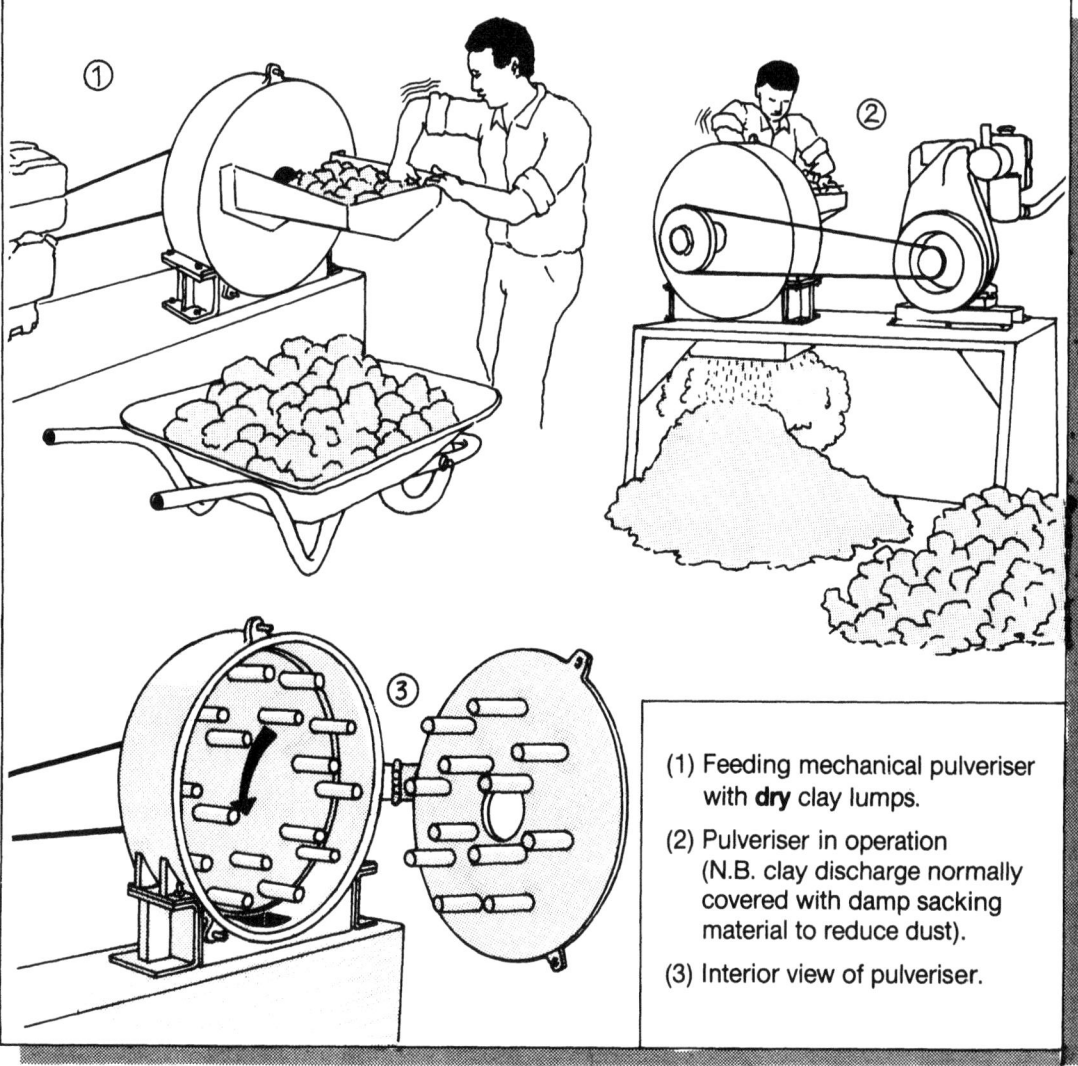

(1) Feeding mechanical pulveriser with **dry** clay lumps.

(2) Pulveriser in operation (N.B. clay discharge normally covered with damp sacking material to reduce dust).

(3) Interior view of pulveriser.

Figure 6.3

rate of production, owing to inefficiencies in the feeding system. Two tonnes of material is enough to make 800 liners, which means that the machine will be used only once every few weeks. The pin mill is expensive, US$5000–$6000, but will last for years without major maintenance. The machine has a hinged door for easy cleaning.

A clay crusher should be professionally manufactured; there are a number of features not shown in the sketch which are vital for trouble-free operation. For example, a series of scrapers and an internal fan behind the rotating disk should be installed to protect the taper-roller bearings and keep the disk rotating freely inside the drum. Appendix C gives sources of this type of machinery, both in Kenya and Europe. Because the clay crusher is not essential and will be economical only for a limited number of producers, engineering drawings are not part of the technology package.

Heavy duty hammer mills designed for grinding grain can also be used. They will produce a very fine clay, but must be operated at a slower speed than normal. They need more power than a pulveriser. A hammer mill is more suitable for use with very hard, dense clay, while a pin mill works best on lighter clay. A pin mill can tolerate up to 8 to 9 per cent moisture, while clay passed through a hammer mill must be bone dry.

Screening crushed clay and mixing with other materials

A business should store sufficient quantities of the pulverized material required for the clay mixture to last for at least two weeks of normal production. (Dry clay is much easier to measure than wet clay.) On the other hand, it is not advisable to store more than a month's supply of pulverized clay because, if left too long in a large pile, it will compact and form lumps.

Before being measured, the clay must be screened. In Figure 6.4 two people shake a small (20kg capacity) sieve between them,

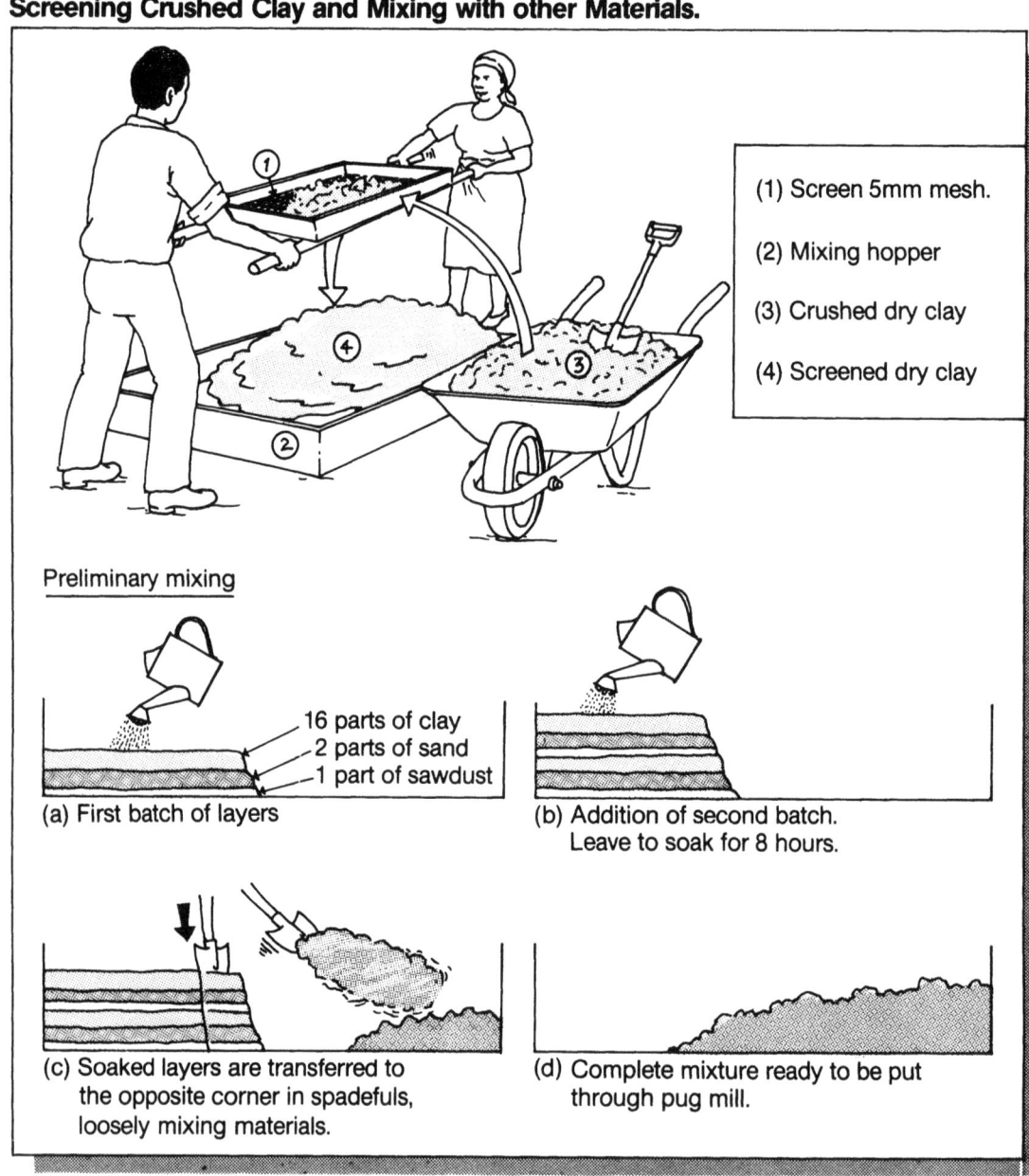

Figure 6.4

and the powder falls into a mixing hopper. Another method of screening involves resting a larger sieve between two trestles or oil drums, and agitating the pulverized clay with a wooden hoe. This creates much less dust.

If clay is sieved in the manner illustrated, or in a confined space, workers must be provided with face masks. Breathing in clay dust causes silicosis, an irreversible lung disease. Daily exposure to large amounts of dust can lead to death within a few years, and bronchitis in a matter of months.

Once the clay and other materials are sieved, they are measured to comply with the selected formula. Here, 16 parts of clay by volume are mixed with 2 parts of sand and 1 part of sawdust. First, the sawdust is laid out in a thin layer, and then the sand is spread on top. The clay is then added, and the whole mass sprinkled with 80 litres of water. Another mixture is then prepared in the same way, spread on top of the first. As many as four mixtures can be prepared in this way. The mixture should be allowed to rest for at least 8 hours to enable the water to penetrate the entire mass of clay and break down any small lumps that remain. Clay which is 'soured' in this fashion will be far more plastic and workable, and far less liable to cracking in drying. Wambugu prepares up to 2t of material in this way, enabling it to sour for several days.

After souring, the material is moved in spadefuls from one end of the hopper to the other, loosely mixing the ingredients into a body. At this point, the clay has the consistency of damp sawdust. When shovelling, it is important to cut vertically through the mass of material to ensure correct proportions in the mixture. The clay mixture can again be left for several hours, to further improve the plasticity of the final product.

Mixing clay manually

Manual mixing of clay is hard work (Figure 6.5). It will take a single individual a full working day to make enough clay for 100 liners. This does not include the time needed to dry crush the clay.

When the damp mixture is ready in the hopper, the worker starts at one end and pushes down through the mass of clay with one foot and moves the clay to one side. The entire mass is worked through at least twice, and water added as needed to ensure proper consistency.

Mixing Clay Manually

Mixing clay, sand, sawdust and water by foot.

Figure 6.5

It is a good idea to have a few buckets of dry-mixed material available in case the body becomes too wet. Dry material is added to return the mixture to the correct consistency. A manual mixing method should be used until stove sales are sufficient to justify the purchase of a pugmill or other mechanical mixing equipment.

It is important to control tightly the measurement of materials, and to constantly emphasize the need to stick to the listed mixture. The proportions for the mixture should be posted in large letters on the wall of the mixing room, for example:

Clay mixture (Buckets)	
Clay	16
Sand	2
Sawdust	1
Water	4

If liners suddenly start to crack in drying or in the kiln, the first factor to check is the mixing process, not the materials themselves.

If you are recycling old clay liners and adding them to the mixture, these should be counted as a mixture, not as pure clay (they already contain sand and sawdust).

Mixing Clay by Machine (Loading and Pressing)

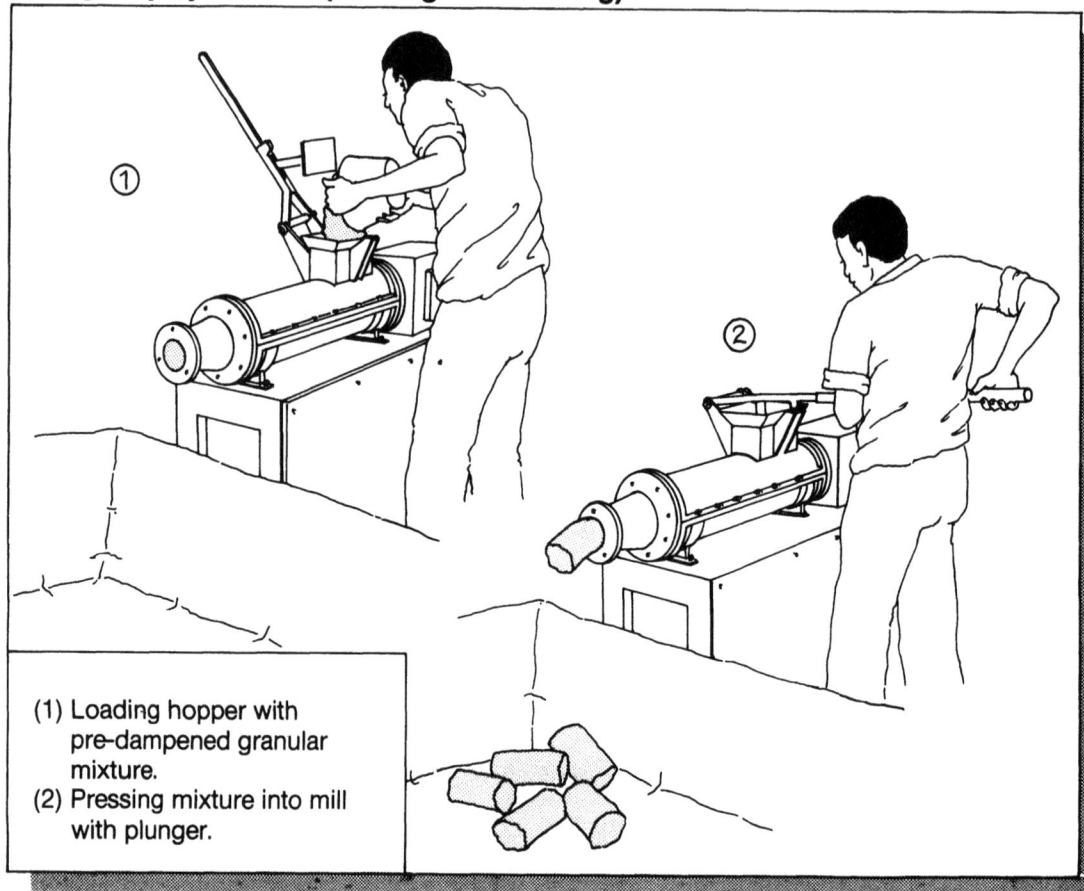

(1) Loading hopper with pre-dampened granular mixture.
(2) Pressing mixture into mill with plunger.

Figure 6.6

Mixing clay by machine

As mentioned above, any stove business should begin by manually mixing a clay body. Although we discuss pugmills and other mechanical mixing equipment in this manual, these are not essential. Whether a business wants or needs one will depend on the scale of production and the local market for jikos.

Several machines can be used to mechanically mix the prepared clay body. The most common is a pugmill, shown in Figure 6.6, which both mixes and extrudes the clay. A pugmill mixes clay far more thoroughly than any manual system and breaks down any lumps that have remained through the souring period.

Clay body material is passed into the hopper on the right-hand side of the pugmill, and either self-feeds into the machine or is pressed by a plunger. The granular material prepared according to the process described in this manual will drop naturally into the pugmill without assistance. However, using the plunger nearly doubles the capacity of the mill and allows materials to pass through faster. A plunger is usually required to feed plastic clay into the mill.

Granular clay is mixed inside the machine and extruded through a reduced opening, which compacts the clay into a plastic form. In other types of clay mixers, water and powdered materials are directly loaded into a large bowl and formed into clay by the action of rotating knives. These mixers are usually used in conjunction with a pugmill which tends to make the clay more dense and forces out air which is mixed into the body. Mixing air into the body increases the insulation properties of the finished liner by creating microscopic voids in the mass of the clay. It also helps the liner resist cracking. Two American companies, Bluebird and Soldner (see Appendix C), manufacture mixers which are capable of producing 300–400kg per hour.

A baker's dough mixer is an excellent substitute for a commercial clay mixer, and can be used without any modification. Although a new dough mixer sells for about double the cost of a pugmill, used machines can often be purchased very cheaply. In Togo, and perhaps in other countries, dough mixers are produced locally from scrapped car parts, and are available on a cost-for-service basis. Because dough is a little softer than clay and uses less power, the mixer should always be set at the slowest speed. Many commercial potteries in England use dough mixers as standard equipment. Given an occasional greasing, these machines will give years of trouble-free service.

General View and Interior of Pugmill

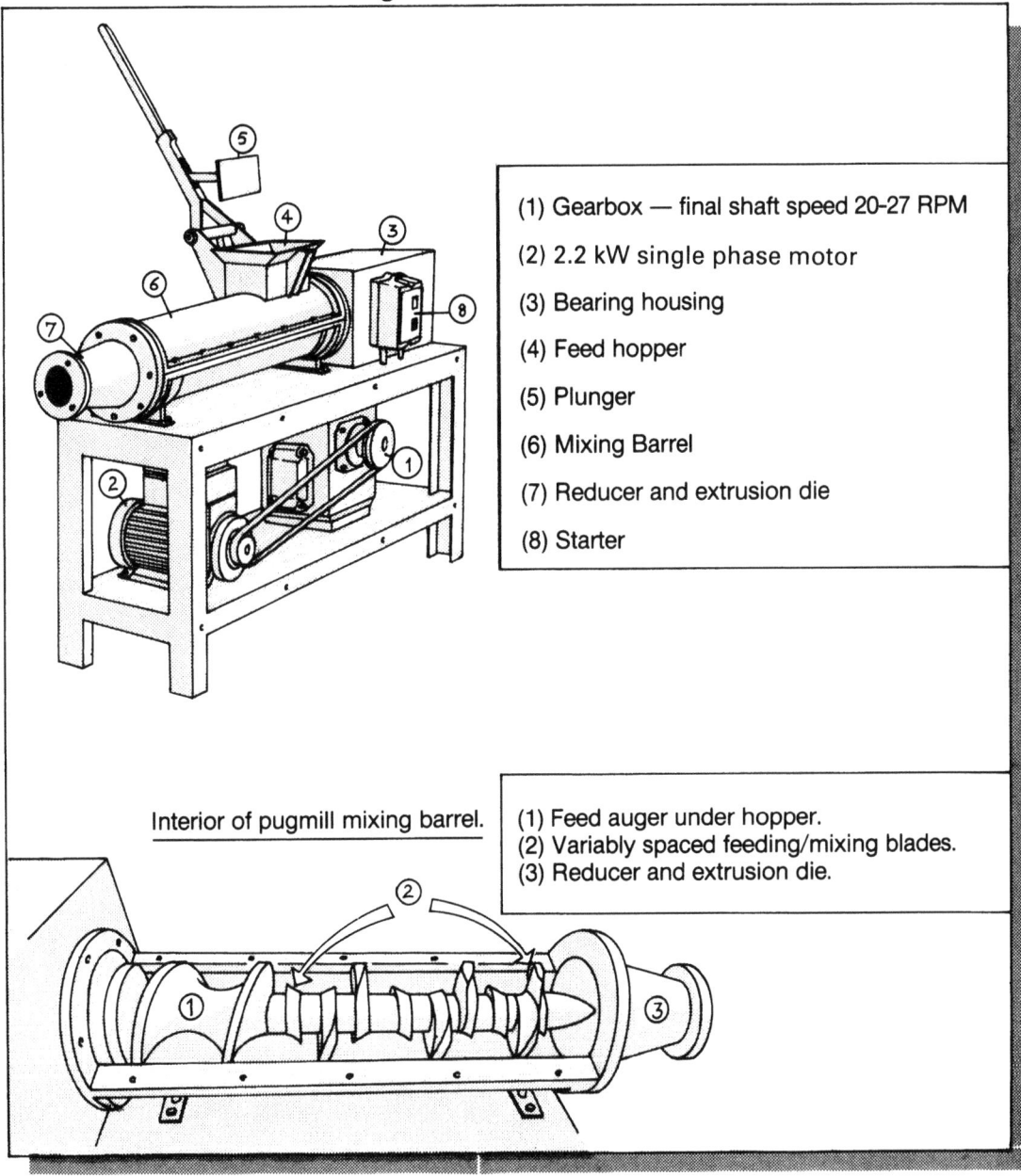

(1) Gearbox — final shaft speed 20-27 RPM

(2) 2.2 kW single phase motor

(3) Bearing housing

(4) Feed hopper

(5) Plunger

(6) Mixing Barrel

(7) Reducer and extrusion die

(8) Starter

Interior of pugmill mixing barrel.

(1) Feed auger under hopper.
(2) Variably spaced feeding/mixing blades.
(3) Reducer and extrusion die.

Figure 6.7

General view and interior of pugmill

Figure 6.7 shows the pugmills built in Kenya specifically for use in stove-making. Only a few manufacturers make equipment suited to this scale, that is production between 500kg and 1t an hour. Most ceramic companies make pugmills that are either very small and flimsy, with a low production rate, or very large, capable of making several tonnes of clay an hour. Most commercial machines have specialized gearboxes and blade-castings that cannot easily be replaced. Appendix C lists the names and addresses of suppliers in England, Australia and the United States who make suitable equipment.

A pugmill consists of a mixing barrel in which a rigid shaft rotates at 15–25rpm, depending on the power available, and the diameter of the barrel. The shaft has an auger, located underneath the feed-hopper, and a number of blades pitched to the same angle as the feed auger. These blades can be fixed at different positions according to the performance needed from the mill. If thorough mixing is needed, the blades can be spaced widely at the input end of the shaft and more closely at the outlet. For high output and less mixing, the blades can be spaced closely at the input end, and further apart at the outlet. In both cases, at least two blades are placed opposite each other at the outlet, rather like a propeller, to ensure proper extrusion and compression of the final mixture.

The machine shown here has a shaft speed of 22rpm, driven by a 2.2kW motor, and a barrel diameter of 165mm. The auger and blades have an effective diameter of 155mm, leaving a 5mm radial clearance between the blades and the casing to ensure that material does not merely rotate inside the barrel. The reducer outlet is 110mm in diameter. A common ratio between the internal diameter of the barrel and the diameter of the reducer outlet is 3:2. It is important that the shaft stops at least 150mm from the end of the outlet so that the clay bonds into a solid mass, without a hole down the centre. A machine built to these specifications with a 130mm pitch to the auger and 9 mixing blades will have a capacity of at least 500kg when self-feeding, and 950kg when manually fed by the plunger.

High-quality machines use bronze or stainless-steel shafts to avoid corrosion and contamination of the clay with iron oxide, but this high standard is not necessary for a liner-making pugmill.

In actual use, the machine operates below its rated capacity due to efficiency losses in feeding. Thus, realistically, a pugmill of the recommended capacity processes about 350kg per hour, enough to make 100 liners. Used for only two hours a day, it can process enough clay to make 1000 liners a week. The spare capacity allows for expansion of output as needed.

General layout of jigger-jolley liner moulding machine and moulding tools

The jigger-jolley machine illustrated in Figure 6.8 is the original moulding machine developed by ATI for use in Wambugu's factory in Kenya. It has worked without breakdown for three and a half years, and is the model for machines which are working in Sudan, Uganda, Rwanda and Togo. The Rwandan machine is hand-powered, but is essentially the same. The only change made in later machines is the addition of a counter-shaft to allow for more conveniently sized pulleys and a slower rate of rotation. (Wambugu's machine has a wheelhead rotation speed of 220rpm, which is marginally too fast.)

The Engineering Drawing Set (pp. 75–98) contains detailed parts drawings, exploded views and orthogonals of the jigger-jolley. It is not possible to buy a machine of this type from a ceramic supplier because its use for making liners is highly specialized. Normal jigger-jolley machines use hundreds of removable plaster moulds for different pottery products. Plaster promotes rapid drying, enabling the finished piece to be removed from the mould after about an hour. Both the pot and the mould are removed as a whole from the jigger-jolley. The pot is later taken from the mould when the plaster has drawn enough water from the clay to make it stiff enough to be safely handled. Because the stove liner is more than 20mm thick it is inherently stiff and can be released immediately from a single metal mould without drying. For this reason it is easier to make the jigger-jolley than to buy one from a supplier and modify the design.

The jigger-jolley has a turntable (5) designed to rotate at 180rpm in an anticlockwise direction. The mould (4) is locked to the turntable by means of three L-shaped bayonet lugs. A swinging arm (8) to which the moulding blade (1) is attached descends into the mould to form the liner. The machine uses a 0.5kW single-phase electric motor. This is started

General Layout of "Jigger-Jolley" Liner Moulding Machine & Moulding Tools.

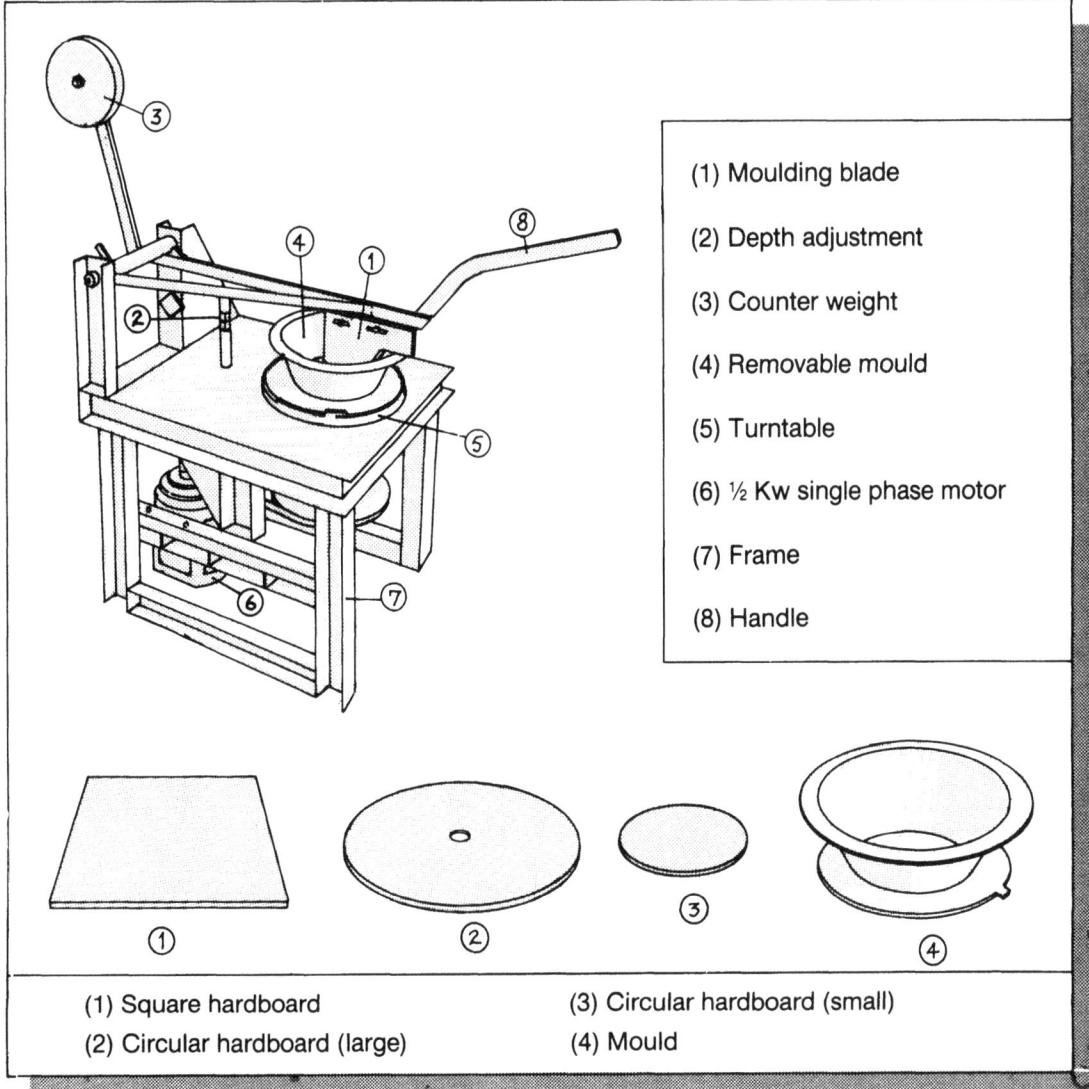

(1) Moulding blade
(2) Depth adjustment
(3) Counter weight
(4) Removable mould
(5) Turntable
(6) ½ Kw single phase motor
(7) Frame
(8) Handle

(1) Square hardboard
(2) Circular hardboard (large)
(3) Circular hardboard (small)
(4) Mould

Figure 6.8

automatically and stopped by a microswitch, activated by lowering and raising the swinging arm. The machines are designed to accept a wide range of moulds, but in East Africa it has been found practical to restrict the number of moulds to three standard sizes.

The other moulding tools are boards 1, 2 and 3, used to remove the liner from the mould and for drying. The two circular boards are best made from 6–8mm marine plywood, and the square board from hardboard (Masonite). It is only necessary to make one of each of the circular boards, but at least 150 square boards will be needed. The circular boards are only used to release the liner from the mould. The square boards are used to support the liners while they dry for a couple of days. Enough square boards should be made to cover at least two days' production. The use of these boards is shown in Figure 6.11.

Preparation and fitting of mould onto turntable

If the mould is used without any preparation, the liners will stick to the metal walls and it will be impossible to release the finished work from the machine. Thus, it is necessary first to coat

Preparation and Fitting of Mould onto the Turntable

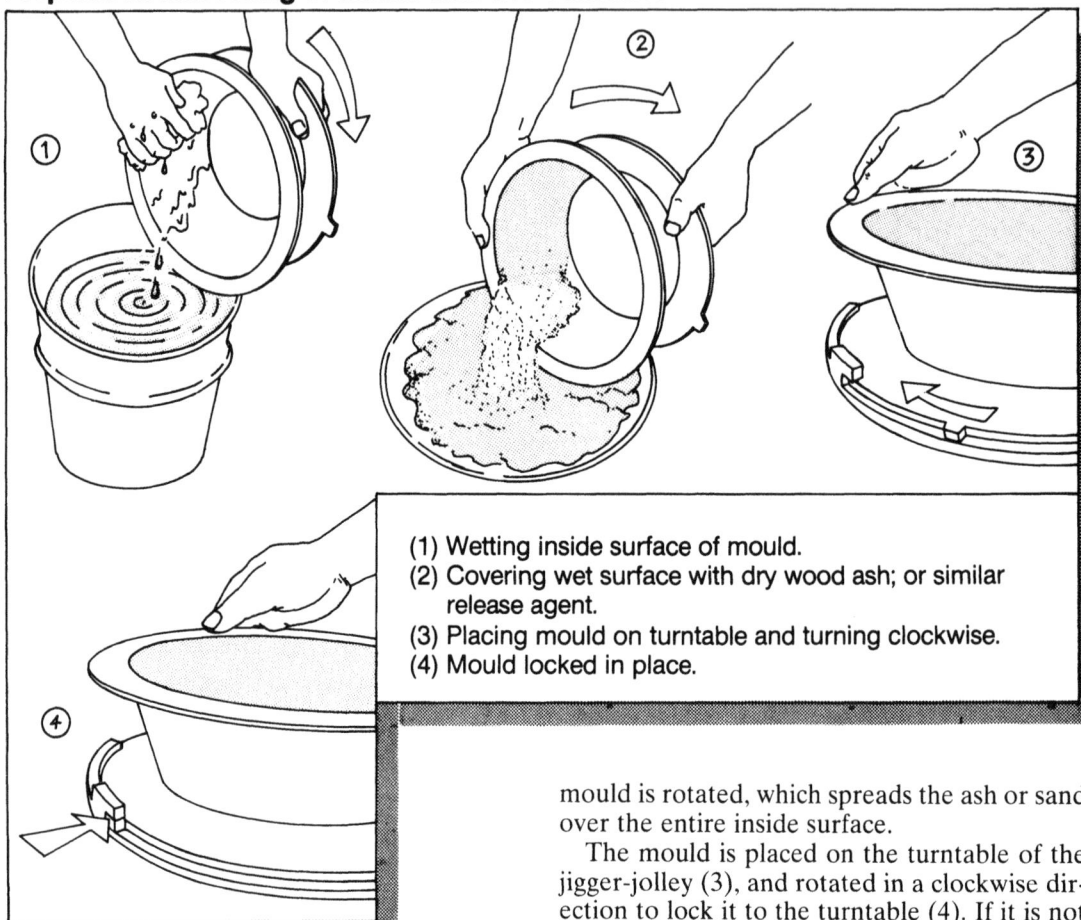

(1) Wetting inside surface of mould.
(2) Covering wet surface with dry wood ash; or similar release agent.
(3) Placing mould on turntable and turning clockwise.
(4) Mould locked in place.

Figure 6.9

the walls of the mould with a release agent to prevent the wet clay from sticking. The two best agents used in East Africa are sieved wood-ash (Kenya, Rwanda, Uganda) or fine, dry sand (Sudan). Coarse sand does not work well, and must pass through at least a 30mm mesh screen to be usable. Wood-ash is best prepared by screening and soaking it in a tub of water for a week, stirring occasionally, and then drying. Some types of wood-ash are caustic and, unless prepared in this way, can cause skin burns.

When the operator is ready to make a liner a damp sponge should be used to wet the inside surface of the mold (see Figure 6.9(1). The mould should not be so wet that water runs off. The mould is then laid on a bed of fine sand or wood-ash. A handful of the release agent is sprinkled on the lower inside surface (2). The mould is rotated, which spreads the ash or sand over the entire inside surface.

The mould is placed on the turntable of the jigger-jolley (3), and rotated in a clockwise direction to lock it to the turntable (4). If it is not locked, the mould may fly off the turntable when the forming blade is lowered.

When the mould is set in place a small amount of sand or wood-ash is sprinkled on the visible face of the turntable (the mould has no bottom) to prevent the clay from sticking to the wheelhead.

After every four or five liners, clean the undersurface of the mould. This will prevent sand or clay from building up, making it difficult for the locking lugs to engage.

Steps in moulding a liner

After the mould is locked to the wheelhead, and coated with an appropriate release agent, the clay is thrown firmly into the cavity. The wheelhead is rotated first by hand, and the clay is beaten into a rough bowl shape with the fist (Figure 6.10(1). This not only reduces the amount of work that the forming blade needs to do but helps to force the clay against the metal walls of the mould.

When the clay is ready for moulding, a few

Steps in Moulding a Liner

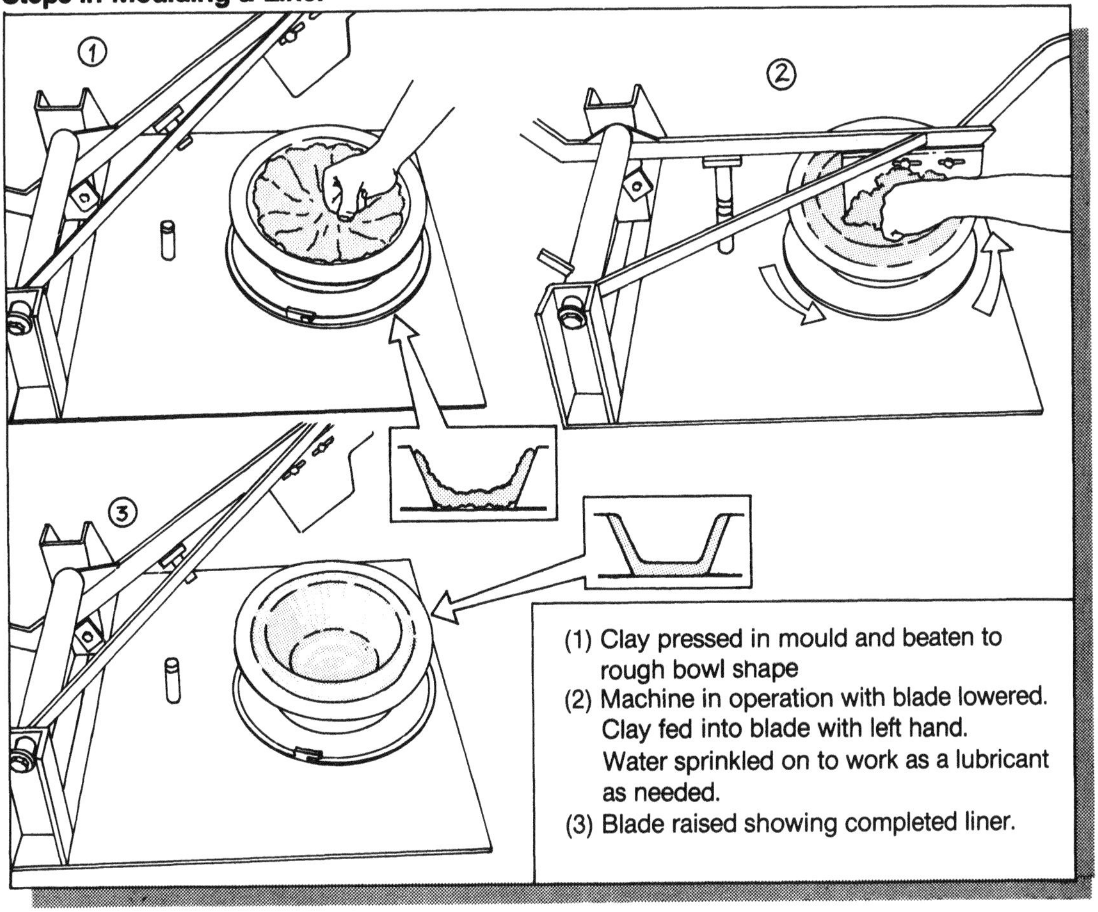

(1) Clay pressed in mould and beaten to rough bowl shape
(2) Machine in operation with blade lowered. Clay fed into blade with left hand. Water sprinkled on to work as a lubricant as needed.
(3) Blade raised showing completed liner.

Figure 6.10

drops of water are sprinkled onto the clay, and the handle lowered into the mould. A microswitch automatically starts the wheelhead rotating. When the blade starts to form the liner, the left hand is used to feed excess clay into the forming blade and occasionally to sprinkle more water into the mould. Sprinkling water on the liner during the moulding process helps to lubricate the clay and stops it from tearing. When the moulding is complete, a few drops of water are allowed to drip into the mould, to give the finished liner a shiny surface (Figure 6.10(3)). When the handle is raised, the jigger-jolley stops working.

To reduce wear on the machine, use the height adjustment on the swinging arm to make sure that the moulding blade descends far enough to make the liner but not so far as to wear out the blade against the rim. When there is no clay in the mould, switch the machine off and bring the handle down. The stop should be adjusted so that there is 0.5–1.0mm clearance between the blade and the rim. This can be set by loosening the locknut and screwing the adjustment screw into its housing so that when the blade is lowered it touches the mould. Four pieces of thick paper are placed between the blade and the mould rim; the adjustment screw is lowered until it hits the stop. Then the locknut is tightened. When the paper is removed, there should be a clear gap of about 1.0mm between the mould and the blade.

The blade must be properly set each time a different size liner is made. It should be possible for a wooden block 22–25mm thickness to fit between the blade and the walls of the mould. It also should fit between the blade and the face of the turntable, to ensure that the liners will all have the same thickness.

Periodically, the moulding blade should be refiled to its original shape. Its edges should retain the original curves and angles ground into the metal when it was made.

As indicated in the Engineering Drawing Set (pp. 74–98), the blade has a curved/angled leading edge to help feed the clay against the walls of the mould. The curved edge will wear away after a few months of use, especially if

Removing the Liner from the Mould

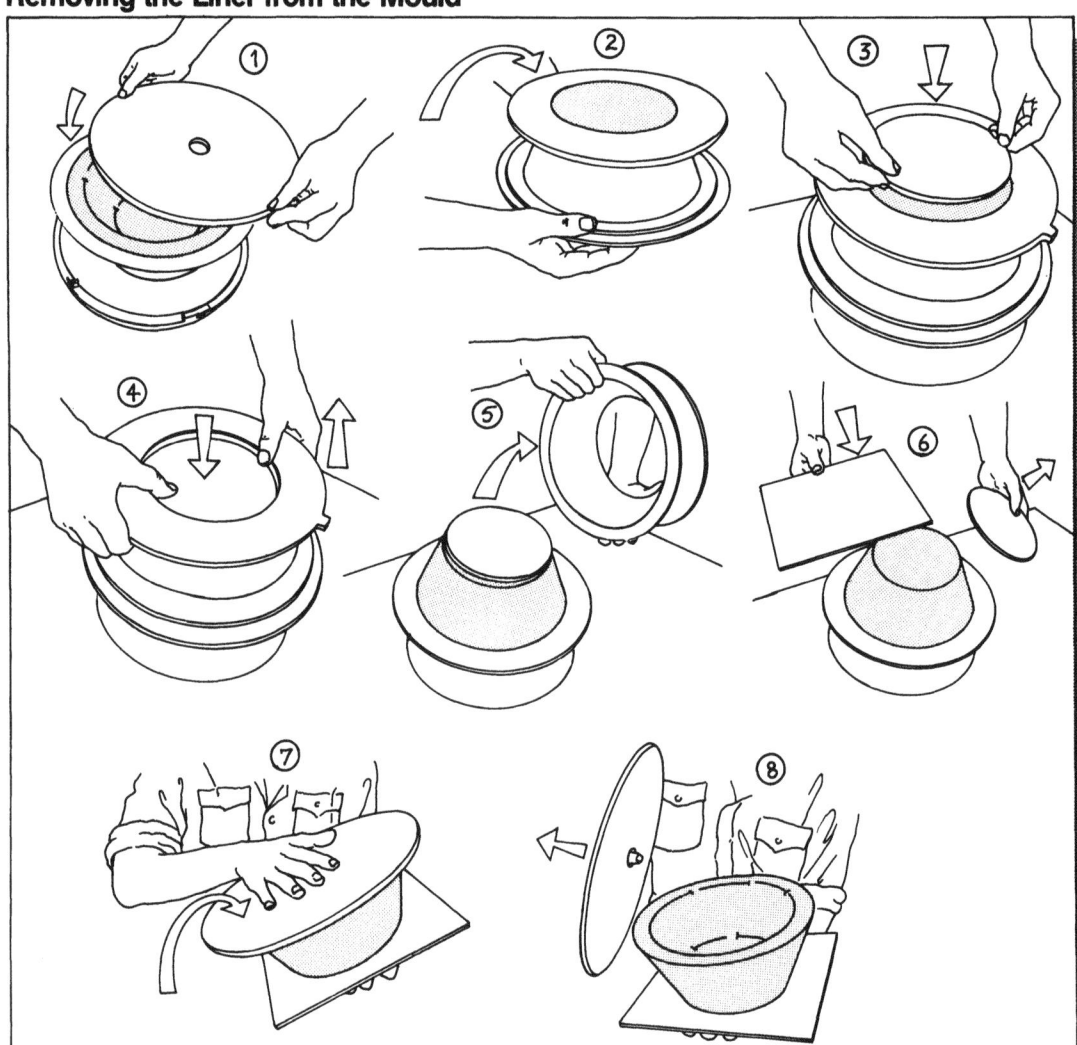

(1) Place wooden disk over mould. Surface of disk sprinkled lightly with wood ash.
(2) Turn upside down
(3) Place small disk on bottom of liner
(4) Press down on disk and lift up on mould.
(5) Remove mould
(6) Put square drying board on bottom of liner
(7) Turn upright
(8) Remove large disk, take liner to drying area. Liner remains on square drying board.

Figure 6.11

there is a lot of sand in the clay. If the blade's leading edge becomes flat the jigger-jolley will lose its efficiency; the liners will be weaker because the clay will not have been sufficiently compressed by the machine.

Removing the liner from the mould

The great advantage of the jigger-jolley is that it makes a regular and smooth liner that is more readily marketable. If at this stage the liner is touched by the hand or dumped upside down on to the ground (as is done in the traditional method) it will be deformed. A lot of subsequent cleaning will be needed to restore its original appearance. The removal method shown here uses the boards (see pp. 49 and 52), to help keep the liner perfectly circular and smooth around the rim.

While the liner and mould are still on the jigger-jolley, the large plywood disk with a hole in its centre is placed over the rim of the mould (Figure 6.11(1). With the mould and the board held tightly together, the mould is twisted sharply in an anticlockwise direction to release the locking lugs. The mould and board, still gripped together, are then turned upside down (2). The circular board and mould are placed on a table surface and the smaller wooden disk is placed on the liner bottom (3). The wooden disk is made to fit inside the bottom of the mould, with a clearance of about 5mm around the circumference.

The mould base is then gripped and lifted up, while downward pressure is maintained on the wooden disk (4). This releases the mould from the liner and leaves the disk on the bottom of the liner (5). The disk is then removed, and a drying-board made of hardboard is placed on the bottom of the liner (6). The whole assembly, including the large disk with a hole in the centre, is then lifted up and turned upside down, returning the liner to an upright position (7). The large disk is then removed (8), and the liner taken on the square hardboard to the drying shelves. It remains on the drying board until it is stiff enough to be handled without deformation. This usually takes one or two days.

This method of removing the liner from the mould may seem complicated, but is actually simple and fast. The resulting improvement in the appearance and roundness of the liner repays the trouble of making the necessary disks.

Drilling grate holes in the liner

The number of holes to be made in the grate varies with the size of the liner. In East Africa the two larger sizes of stove have 19 holes while the smallest has only 14. The layout of these holes is shown in Figure 6.12(3) and (4). It is important to punch the holes so that they are equidistant from each other. Careful examination of the drawings shows that the holes are laid out in a series of equilateral triangles.

At first, laying out the holes in a symmetrical and consistent pattern may seem complicated but if the sequence shown in (3) and (4) is followed it becomes very simple. An experienced worker can punch a complete grate in as little as 30 seconds, although it usually takes about 1 minute.

A simple tool is used to punch the holes. It can be made from galvanized sheet steel 0.8–1.0mm thick. The sheet is roll-formed into a tapered tube, with the smaller end precisely sized to 19mm diameter. Holes punched to this size are large enough to allow ash to drop easily into the grate without letting lumps of charcoal pass through. If the holes are smaller they will tend to clog. The range of acceptable hole sizes is 17–22mm in leather-hard clay; that is clay hard enough to be picked up without deforming but soft enough to allow cutting and punching without cracking or crumbling around the edges of the holes.

The taper of the punch helps the clay which is removed to release without sticking to the inside of the punch. When the grate is drilled the punch is first wetted and then pressed firmly to the bottom of the liner, twisted one quarter turn and withdrawn. The twisting action helps to facilitate release, and ensures that the hole is smooth and circular.

The liners should be punched on a soft surface such as an old inner-tube or piece of old hardboard. This allows the punch to go right through the base without leaving a rim of thin edges, which would restrict the size of the grate holes.

The most common error made even by experienced workers is to punch the holes at an angle. This should be regularly checked before it becomes a habit. Another common problem is a failure to maintain the punch in good order. If pressed down on to small stones which are hidden in the clay, the punch will deform, so it should be inspected daily for this problem.

At this stage the outer edge of the rim should be smoothed. When the liner is removed from the mould the outer edge tends to have thin

Drilling Grate Holes in Liner (Sequence and Number of Holes)

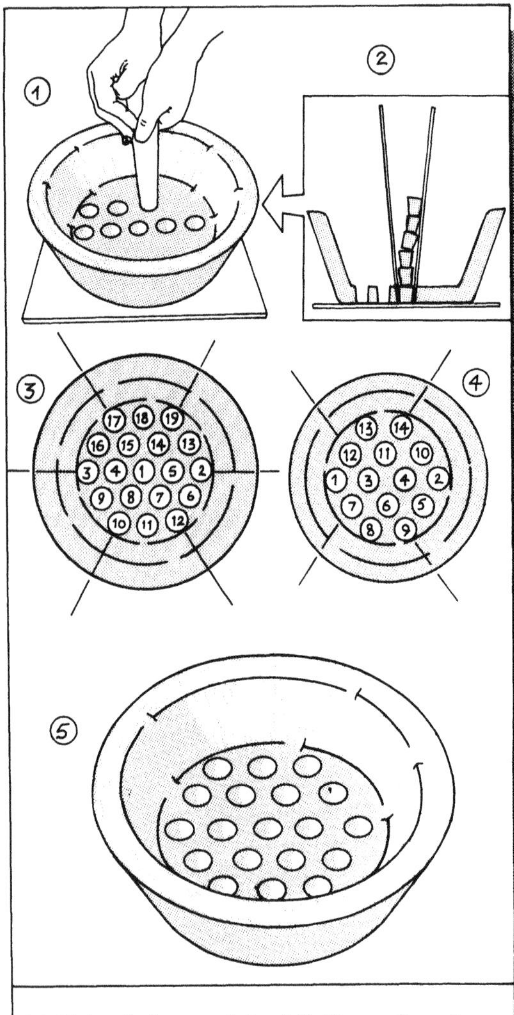

(1) Using hole punch to drill 19mm diameter grate holes. Press down, twist, withdraw.
(2) Section through punch showing action.
(3) Layout of holes for standard liners showing sequence in which holes are punched.
(4) Layout of holes in small liner. Note that holes are equally spaced.
(5) Completed grate of standard liner.

Figure 6.12

pieces of clay sticking out unevenly. These can be removed with a carpenter's roughing tool such as a surform, a flat, 40mm wide blade with a surface like a cheese grater that allows clay to be scraped off the edge. The excess clay passes through dozens of holes in the blade.

Drying liners on racks and in the sun before firing

Drying ceramic products, especially thick-walled pieces such as the KCJ liner, is an art. Proper formulation of the clay greatly reduces the loss rate, but even after the liners are made they must be dried with care. The drying clay must be protected from the sun and the wind.

The drying-racks shown in Figure 6.13 allow the liners to dry individually, and are made from poles and off-cuts of wood. There is a great temptation to stack the liners on top of each other when they are leather-hard, to save space, but experience has shown that losses of up to 20 per cent in drying are incurred if the liners are stacked up before they are dry. The liners are left on their boards even after punching until they are quite hard. Then they are again laid out singly until they are completely dry. A completely dry liner has a distinctive tone when tapped with a knuckle.

The drying-sheds have open sides, but plastic sheets can be rolled down to protect the liners from wind and direct exposure to the hot sun. In hot, arid climates it is a good idea to construct a ceiling. In addition, large porous water jars set around the drying-shed will maintain a moist atmosphere and slow down the drying process.

When the liners are ready to go into the kiln, it is a good idea to lay them in the sun for at least four hours before loading them into the kiln, even if they are dry. This preheats the liners and drives off any moisture that may have been reabsorbed by the clay after drying. A dry clay article can absorb surprising amounts of moisture from the air, up to 6 per cent by weight.

Before the liners are placed in the kiln, they should be inspected for cracks. Minor surface cracks can be filled with a stiff clay after dampening the surface of the liner. Cracks that are more than 2–3mm deep cannot be repaired and the liner should be rejected and recycled into clay.

The underside of the liners should also be inspected to ensure that the grate holes are open and that thin rims of clay do not restrict the hole size. Any such rims should be removed by inserting a tapered piece of steel flat-bar into the hole and twisting.

Drying Liners on Racks and in the Sun before Firing

(1) Covered drying racks. Note that liners are dried individually and not stacked.
(2) Liners laid out to pre-heat in the sun just before firing.

Figure 6.13

CHAPTER 7

The kiln

History of the Tigoni kiln

The updraught kiln which is illustrated in this manual was first built at Tigoni in Kenya, as part of a training course for Sudanese stove-makers. It is able to fire 440 liners using the same amount of fuel and in the same time as a smaller kiln that only holds 118 liners. This kiln has been fired on average 5–6 times a month for three years. The firebars in the kiln have been replaced once, and firemouth brick repairs have been carried out twice. Losses in firing are usually less than 1 per cent, although 5–10 per cent breakage can be expected if the liners are fired before they are thoroughly dry. The same kiln design is used in Sudan, Rwanda and Uganda.

Why an updraught kiln?

There are two main types of kiln: updraught and downdraught. In an updraught kiln, the gases start from the bottom of the kiln and exit at the top, passing directly through the pots or liners (ware) stacked inside the firing chamber. In a downdraught kiln, the gases start at the bottom of the kiln, and bypass the ware *en route* to the top of the kiln. The gases are then drawn down through the ware, and into the chimney flues which usually run under the floor of the kiln. In both types of kiln, the gases then go to a chimney. In an updraught kiln, this is usually a natural extension of the firing chamber while in a downdraught kiln the chimney is usually separate from the main body of the kiln.

We recommend using an updraught kiln to fire the liners because:

o A downdraught kiln requires twice as many firebricks as an updraught kiln.
o At the relatively low temperatures needed to fire liners a downdraught kiln uses more fuel than an updraught kiln. In an experiment in Rwanda, substituting an updraught kiln for a downdraught kiln resulted in a 60 per cent fuel saving.
o Although temperature is more evenly distributed in a downdraught kiln, this is only significant at very high temperatures. Carefully packing and closing down an updraught kiln at the end of a firing will result in comparable uniformity in temperature.

A downdraught kiln to fire liners would only be justified if it is also needed to fire other ceramic items at temperatures higher than 1150°C.

Loading the kiln

The kiln is loaded in stacks of liners which reach from the floor to the roof. As many as 20 liners can be stacked in this way, although 16 is more usual. Stacking the liners top-to-toe also helps keep the rims flat and prevents warping. If the liners are stacked in a jumble, or in staggered layers like bricks, the flow of gases will be uneven and restricted, leading to overfiring in some places, underfiring in others and warping. The evenness of heat distribution in a firing depends largely on the way in which the kiln is packed.

Figure 7.1 shows how the floor layer is arranged. The liners are set in such a way that one stack starts with a liner upside down, with the adjacent liner the right way up. The interlocking stacks save a lot of space and stabilize the pack, as seen in the second drawing. The liners should be laid out on the floor to avoid blocking the flue openings. If the openings are restricted, the liners blocking the flue will be overfired, while those in the general area normally heated by the flue will be underfired.

Some kiln users have found that the bottom layer is always overfired, especially when hardwoods are used as a fuel, because they tend to have short flames and concentrate heat around the firebox. This problem can be reduced by burning softwoods such as pine or by leaving a layer of old, unusable liners to form a false floor.

It is important to stack the liners evenly. If the kiln is stacked very high on one side and is left half empty on the other, the firing will be uneven. If there are not enough liners to fill the kiln, they should be stacked to an even level, and shards put across the top layer, to confine the heat to the mass of liners.

When the kiln is loaded, the door is built without mortar, as in the interlocking brick pattern shown in the final drawing. When it is closed up, a 50:50 mixture of sand and clay is smeared

Loading the Kiln

Figure 7.1

over the joints between the door bricks to prevent a leakage of gases during the firing.

It is a good idea to keep one brick loose to be able to observe the interior of the kiln during the firing. This brick should be halfway up the door since an updraught kiln is usually hotter at the bottom than the top. When the bottom layer of liners is red-hot, the upper rows may not glow at all.

Firing the kiln

No two kilns will perform alike. Hot areas in one kiln may be cool in another of the same design. When the general characteristics of a kiln are known, it is possible to compensate for these problems.

Packing

In an updraught kiln, heat tends to concentrate at the bottom, close to the fireboxes, and in loosely packed areas. Even packing of the kiln is generally important, but if there is a persistent cool spot, pack the kiln looser in that area and below. Where there are hot spots, the kiln should be packed more tightly.

Starting the firing

Once the kiln is packed firing can begin. Care in the early stages of firing will greatly affect the loss rate. Clay contains two kinds of water: water mixed into the clay, which evaporates during drying (this will boil at 100°C); and water chemically combined in the clay which can be driven off explosively only at a much higher temperature, about 230°C. If the temperature rises too fast at either of these points, a lot of breakage will occur. Usually, when water boils and is driven off as steam, large deep flakes will be blown away from the walls of the liners. This is a sign that the temperature was raised too fast.

It is a good idea, therefore, to begin firing very slowly at both fireboxes. Although the fireboxes have firebars, small fires can be started on the ground at the mouth of the firebox. After burning steadily at a low flame for a couple of hours, these fires will have thoroughly warmed the kiln and driven off the remaining moisture in the liners. At this point, the wood can be stacked and burned on top of the firebars, as shown in Figure 7.2(1).

Firing the Kiln

(1) Feeding with wood.

(2) Ending the firing — closing.

Figure 7.2

Fuel

The type of wood burned is important in firing a kiln. Softwoods are generally best. Although softwoods have a lower heat value than hardwoods, they give up their heat more easily and create longer flames. The best softwoods for this purpose are pine and eucalyptus. It is also important to use *dry wood*. Dry wood provides almost double the heat of damp, wet wood. It is a good idea to cut the wood into convenient lengths, less than 10cm thick, and stack them around the kiln for future use. The heat from the kiln will dry out the wood, which can then be stacked off the floor in a sheltered store.

Stoking

Be careful not to overload the fireboxes with wood. If not enough air is reaching the fire, the wood will burn inefficiently. It is not necessary to stuff the firebox. It should be filled to no more than 60 per cent of its height above the firebars. Occasionally, the glowing coals should be raked from below the firebars, whenever they reach more than half the height from the floor. Some coals and ash should be left in the bottom of the firebox to help in preheating the air before it reaches the main body of the fire.

Steadily stoking the firebox without overloading it is important. If the wood is allowed to burn down, the temperature in the kiln will drop rapidly. If the fire is not properly fed, the temperature can drop 100°C in 5 minutes; it takes as much as 30 minutes of stoking to recover from this temperature drop.

Air control

The best way to judge combustion is to observe the colour of the flames once the kiln is hot. If the flames are bright, with a bluish tinge, enough air is entering the kiln. If more air goes into the kiln than is needed to support combustion, it will have a cooling effect. If the flames are rushing into the kiln and appear to be blue, the kiln operator should reduce the size of the chimney opening with a sheet of metal until the flames begin to turn more yellow. When this happens, open the chimney just enough to get rid of the yellow flame and restore the blue flame. If the flames are yellow and 'lazy', not enough air is reaching the fire. This can be remedied either by allowing more air into the firebox by removing some fuel, or opening the chimney by withdrawing the iron sheet.

The fire should be stoked evenly from both sides of the kiln until the correct temperature is reached. Judging the correct temperature is the most important part of the firing: if it is too low, the liners will be too weak; if it is too high they will be too brittle. The ideal temperature range appears to be 750–900°C, depending on the type of clay used. Red clays can be fired at the lower range, while lighter clays need to be fired at higher temperatures.

Judging the final temperature and closing down

An updraught kiln has a very uneven temperature distribution while the firing is in progress. Liners just above the firebox will be a strong orange-red while the liners at the top of the kiln will not show signs of any colour. The manner in which the firing is finished is critical in overcoming these differences and standardizing the temperatures from top to bottom.

The colour of the firing is the best way to judge the final temperature. A pyrometer or pyrometric cone will only record the temperature in one part of the kiln. A visual inspection is the best way to judge the overall colour of the firing. To make it easier to observe the colour inside the kiln, the firing can be done after dark.

The most effective way to observe the colour of the firing in this type of kiln is to look down the chimney at an angle across the liners. This is quite safe, as long as the observer keeps his head upwind and well to one side. When the grate holes in the liners on the top of the kiln are outlined by a dull, reflected red heat, it is time to end the firing. This is done by allowing the fire to burn down or raking out the remaining wood as shown in Figure 7.2(2). At the same time, the chimney should be closed completely with a metal sheet or basin. It is a good idea if the basin is put on before the coals are raked out, and the fire allowed to burn for a few minutes at low heat.

When this is done the fireboxes are closed with loose bricks and the kiln is left to cool. Putting a cover over the chimney stops the escape of heat and allows the heat at the bottom of the kiln to rise to the top. Using this system it is possible to achieve a temperature difference between the top and the bottom of this kiln of no more than 50°C, well within acceptable limits.

It is not essential to close the fireboxes to obtain an even distribution of heat. This is done to prevent cracking, which sometimes takes place when cold air comes into contact with red-hot liners.

Tools for Kiln Building

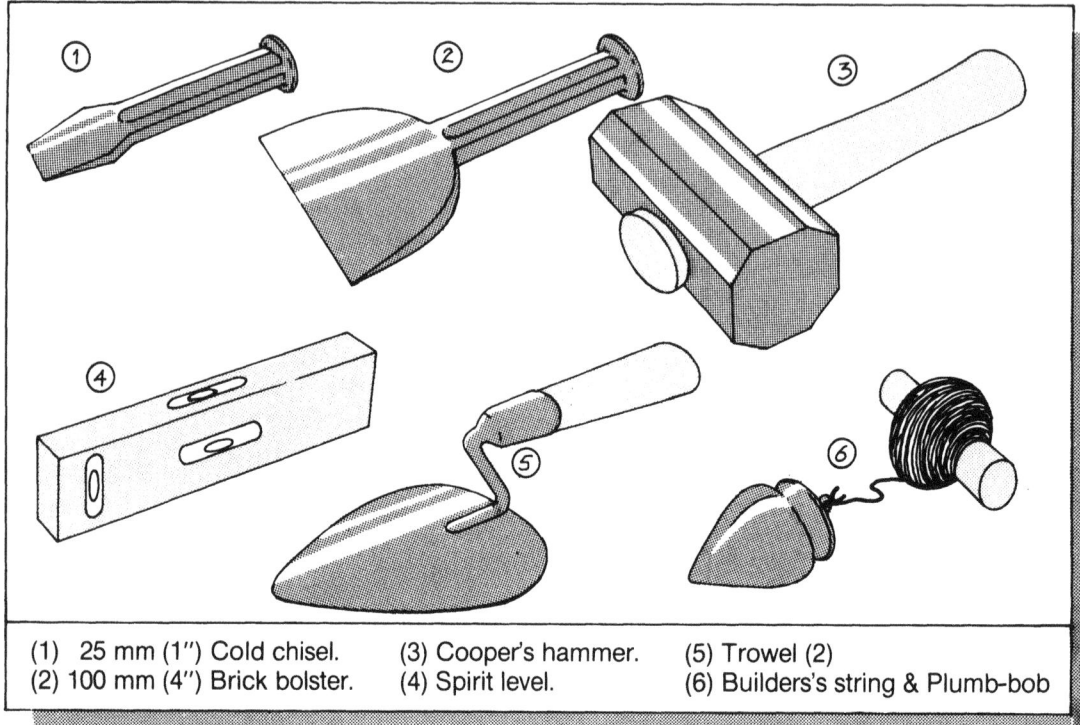

(1) 25 mm (1") Cold chisel.
(2) 100 mm (4") Brick bolster.
(3) Cooper's hammer.
(4) Spirit level.
(5) Trowel (2)
(6) Builders's string & Plumb-bob

Figure 7.3

If liners crack under these conditions, they are probably going to crack in use. A high rate of cracking is an indication that the liners are sub-standard or that the clay mixture is unsatisfactory.

If the fireboxes are left open and the cracking rate in the kiln is no more than 2 per cent, the liners will probably work well in stoves. As a routine test, leave the fireboxes open periodically to expose the liners to stress in the kiln.

An updraught kiln, with a capacity of 420–500 standard liners, can be fired in less than five hours and requires no more than 400kg of dry fuel wood. The kiln may be loaded in the afternoon, and preheated at about 4:00p.m. If full firing begins at 6:00 p.m., the firing will usually be finished at 10:00–10:30 p.m. The kiln is opened the following morning and the liners are in the market by mid-day. Theoretically it is possible to fire the kiln daily, although in practice it has never been fired more than three times in a working week.

Building the kiln

Materials and other requirements

Bricks: The recommended kiln is made from clay building-bricks, which should withstand the firing temperatures needed for liners. Building-bricks made by industrial producers are fired usually to about 1000°C. Higher temperature-resistant bricks may be needed for the firebox, where temperatures can exceed 1150°C. The bricks used to line the roof of the firebox arches and those that form the edges of the flues in to the firing chamber must be tested to make sure that they will not melt at 1200°C. Otherwise the bricks in the firebox flues may melt and will have to be replaced.

The plans of the kiln show standard English building-bricks which measure $9 \times 4.5 \times 3''$ ($228 \times 114 \times 75$mm). If the bricks available are a different size, ignore the number of layers and the number of bricks used in each layer, and try to stick as closely as possible to the critical wall and firebox dimensions. The number of bricks needed will depend on whether the kiln is built to the recommended dimensions, and on the size of the bricks that are available. It will take 2000 standard English building-bricks to build this kiln. If retaining walls are built around the firemouths, 2300–2500 bricks will be needed. If the sizes of the available bricks are very different from the standard English bricks, the following method can be used to calculate the number needed:

Cubic volume (metric) of one standard English brick: ($22.8 \times 11.4 \times 7.5$cm)	1950.00cc
Volume of locally available bricks ($18.5 \times 10.0 \times 5.0$ cm)	925.00cc
Number of local bricks needed to equal volume of one standard English brick (1950/925)	2.108
Number of standard English bricks needed to build the kiln	2300.00
Number of bricks needed to build kiln using local bricks (2300×2.108)	4850.00

Mortar: The mortar used is a mixture of sand and clay in a 1:1 ratio. Water is then mixed in to produce a consistency of stiff building-cement.

Steel: The only metal needed in the kiln is mild steel for the firebars and the dome-retaining band. The firebars are made from 32mm (1¼") mild steel roundbar, joined by 10×32mm (¼ × 1¼") flatbar. The firebars are made in two halves, like ladders, and can be withdrawn from the fireboxes from each side of the kiln. The dome-retaining band is made from 3 strips of 6×75mm (¼ × 3") flatbar, joined by 16mm (⅝") diameter bolts.

Tools: Tools required are shown in Figure 7.3.

Labour and time: It is helpful to have two experienced masons working on the kiln; one should be responsible for construction. They must be supported by two people who work full time on mixing mortar. About 1000 litres of mortar are needed to build the entire kiln. Two additional labourers can be used to carry bricks.

If masons are not available, a completely inexperienced team should be able to build the kiln in six days, while an experienced team can build a kiln in four days if bricks are of convenient sizes and available on site.

Foundation

The kiln does not require a conventional foundation because it is built into a pit that is later back-filled with soil. It is important that the site be well drained so that excessive amounts of energy are not required in every firing to evaporate water that has penetrated the bricks below ground level.

Figure 7.4(1) shows the pit which is dug for the kiln. It is about 1m (39") deep, at least 2.14m (7') wide and about 6m (20') long. The kiln floor should be level and smooth. In the exact centre, a 4m-long piece of 25mm (1") water-pipe is set in a vertical position, braced by string at the four corners of the pit. A spirit-level is used to make sure the pipe is vertical. To measure the radius for the walls, a stiff piece of wire is allowed to rotate freely around the pipe. Figure 7.4(2) shows how the pole and the wire are used to build the first layer of the kiln. Figure 7.4(2) also shows how the firebox channel is established initially from the base of the kiln.

Foundation

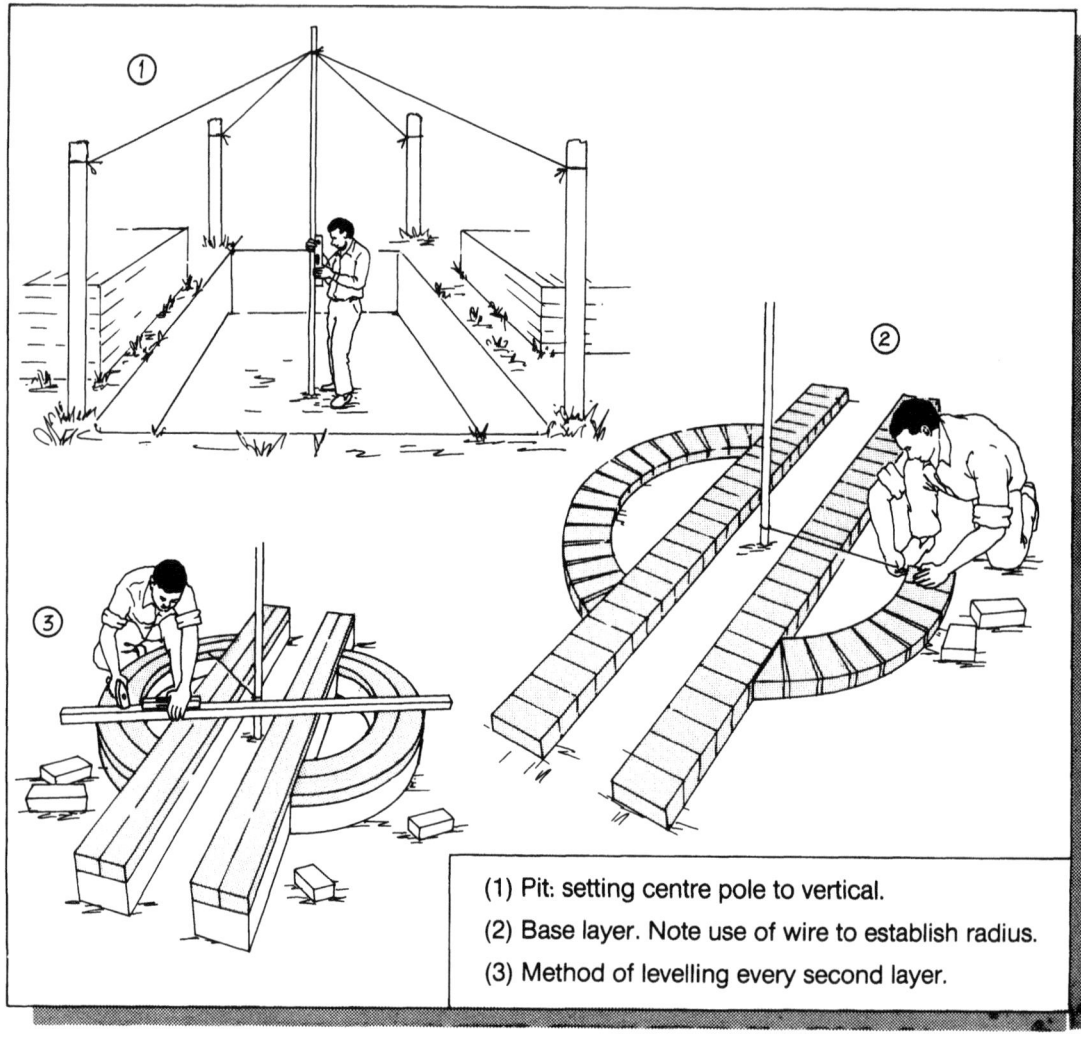

(1) Pit: setting centre pole to vertical.
(2) Base layer. Note use of wire to establish radius.
(3) Method of levelling every second layer.

Figure 7.4

The mortar should be at least 2cm thick, and the brick layer should be set as shown in Figure 7.4(2). A long straight wooden bar is used together with the spirit-level to ensure that the rim is even and built to a constant height. Figure 7.4(3) shows how to keep the walls of the kiln level. By tapping on the straight wooden bar where high spots are noted, the entire wall can be made level. The mortar thickness allows the bricks to be tapped into a lower position. It is important when levelling in this fashion that the bricklayer first identifies the lowest point in the wall and then brings all the other bricks to the same level. Every alternate layer of the kiln should be levelled similarly. If the bricklayer waits until every fourth or fifth layer, it will be difficult to adjust the unevenness without making a mortar layer that is too thick. Since most bricklayers have little experience in building circular walls, they should be very conscientious in using the wire attached to the centre pole and should check regularly the top rim to ensure that it is level.

As shown in Figure 7.4(2), the bottom row of bricks is laid in a radial fashion with the major axes pointing to the centre of the kiln. The next layer is built with the bricks in two concentric rows having axes parallel to the circumference. The firebox bricks are alternated likewise. Building in this fashion makes for an extremely strong wall. When each layer of bricks is finished, the gaps between are packed with a mixture of shards and mortar.

Firebox Construction

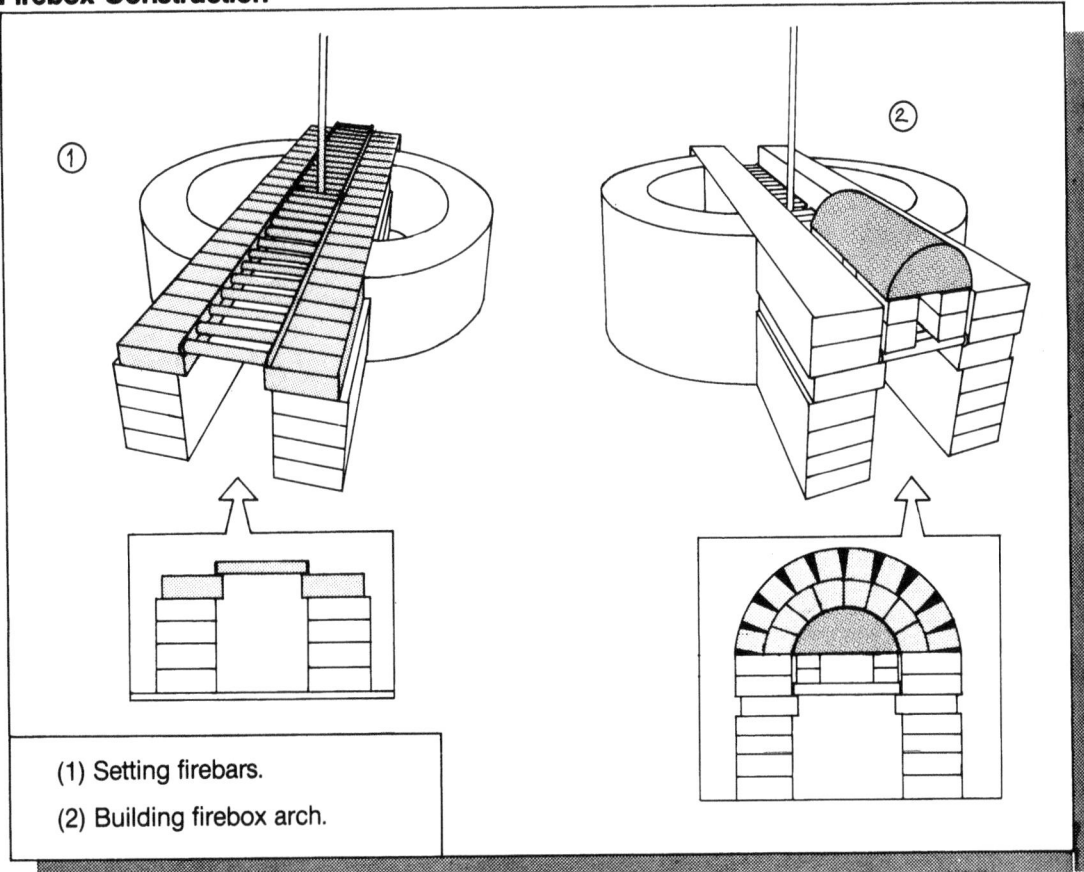

(1) Setting firebars.
(2) Building firebox arch.

Figure 7.5

Firebox construction
When the kiln is about 30cm (12") high, preparations are made to install the firebars. This is done by placing a layer of bricks as shown in Figure 7.5(1), set 19mm (¾") into the firebox. This creates a lip inside the firebox on which the firebars can rest. Construction continues with the firebars in place for another 15cm (6") until the firebox arch is built. To build the arch, use a plywood former constructed around 25mm thick internal wooden bracing. The former is made to a semicircular section, the exact width of the firebox, 280mm (11"), and is about 800mm (32") long. The former is carefully set on bricks so that the bottom edge is level with the top layer of the wall, or a maximum of 1cm above it. Arch bricks are then laid over the wooden former in two layers as shown.

Figure 7.5(2) shows that the inner layer is made from tapered bricks, while the outer layer is made from standard bricks, with the gaps filled in with clay and shards. Both layers can be made from standard bricks but tapered bricks simplify the construction. If tapered bricks are available lay them out with their narrow edges resting on the ground. To see if they are suitable press them together and observe the curve of the arch thus formed. If this arch is the proper size, the arch former should be cut to a similar arc.

When the arch is completed at one end of the kiln the bricks supporting the former are knocked out, and the former allowed to drop down. The arch will remain standing without any additional support. Figure 7.6 shows the kiln with both fireboxes in place.

Preparing Floor Arch Support

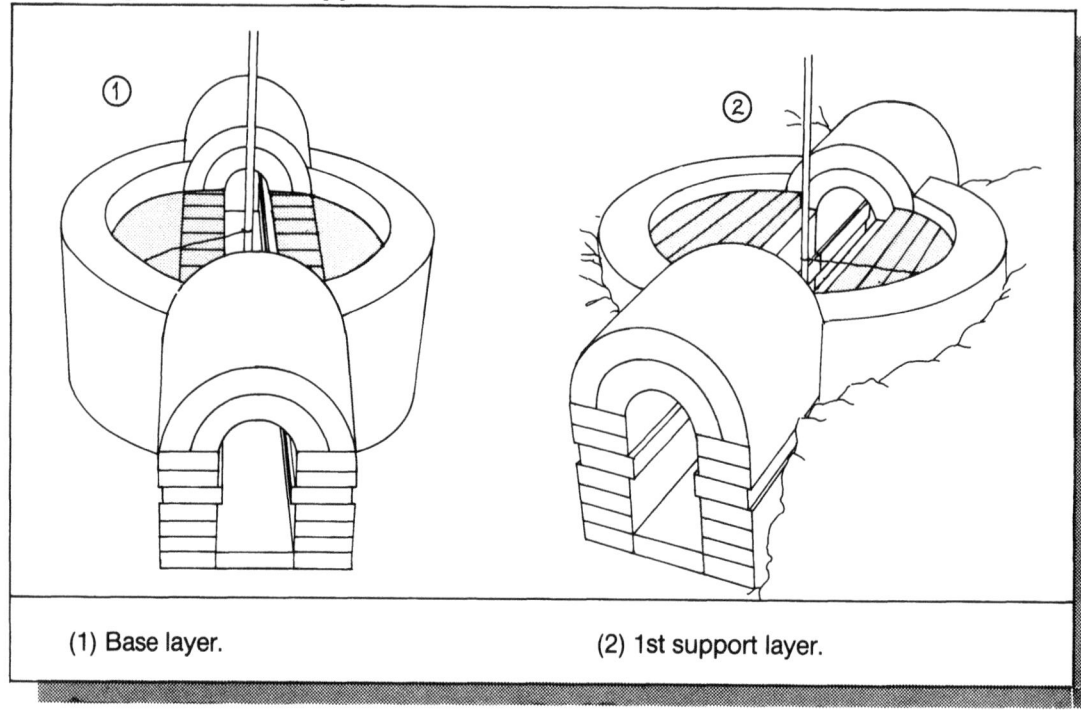

(1) Base layer.

(2) 1st support layer.

Figure 7.6

Preparing floor arch support

Figure 7.6 shows that there is an internal D-shaped space between the walls of the kiln and the fire channel. After the firebox arches have been completed, the outer walls are built up two more layers and the space between the fire channel and outer walls is filled in with a carefully and tightly packed mixture of pottery shards and damp sand. Damp sand is used instead of clay because it will not shrink when it dries, and forms a stable base to support the floor of the kiln. Concrete cannot be used because it will be damaged by the heat of the kiln.

Once the infilling is finished (Figure 7.6(1), a layer of bricks is put across the floor (Figure 7.6(2). This layer is set back from the edge of the fire channel by a further 75mm (3") on each side. This has the effect of widening the fire channel to a total of 430mm (17"). This layer is called the first support layer because it is the first of two brick layers that help support the arches placed over the firebox.

Floor Arch Construction

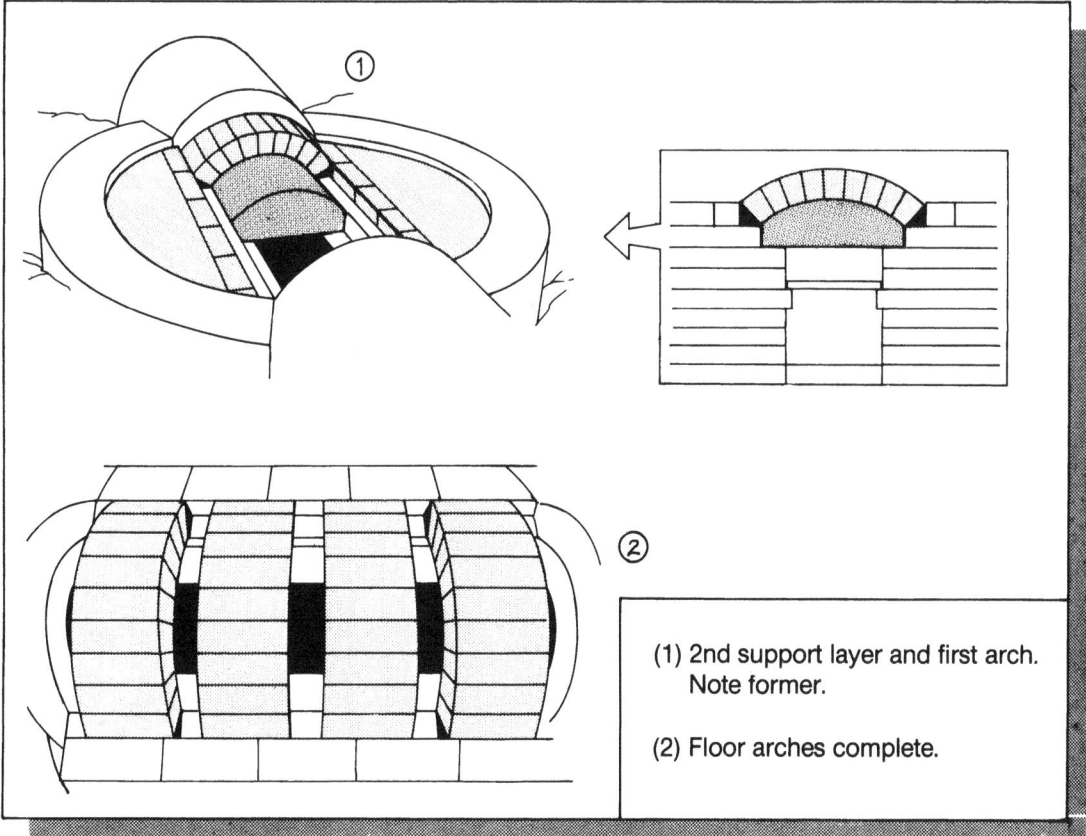

(1) 2nd support layer and first arch. Note former.

(2) Floor arches complete.

Figure 7.7

Floor arch construction

Before the floor arches are put into place another layer of bricks is put on top of the first support layer. This second support layer is set back approximately 75mm from the firebox. The amount this layer is set back is not fixed but varies with the angle needed to support the end bricks that form the floor arches. This can be determined by experimentation. The floor arches are built using a former as in Figure 7.7(1). The former is 430mm (17") wide and 600mm (24") long. The curve on this arch former is such that the bottom of the arch rises in the middle at least 25mm (1") higher than the roof of the firebox arches.

This height difference is important because it helps to prevent flames from flowing backwards out of the firebox.

When two arches have been built at one end of the kiln, the former is removed and slid to the other end so that the remaining two arches can be built. The internal diameter of the kiln is 1370mm (54"). If 228mm (9")-long bricks are used, there will be five equal gaps of about 90mm between the arches and between the arches and the end walls. If the bricks available are shorter than this, trim them to 180mm (7") in length, and leave six (approximately) 78mm (3") gaps between the arches. Whatever number of brick arches are used it is important that the gaps between them be exactly equal, and in no case wider than 90mm (3½").

When all the floor arches are completed, the arch former is trapped and cannot be removed. To remove the former, burn it away. Figure 7.7(2) shows the arches in place with the former removed.

Because the subsequent construction of the kiln requires bricklayers to walk over the floor, it is a good idea to leave the former temporarily in place. If an arch is accidentally disturbed and needs to be rebuilt, the former will still be available. Once the floor is completed, however, the former can be burned.

Construction of flues

When the floor arches are completed single rows of bricks are laid along them to exactly the same width. Figure 7.8(1) shows the half completed brick rows. If the bricks do not match the curve of the arches, fill in the gaps with a mixture of clay, sand and shards. Figure 7.8(2) shows the completed rows, leaving five fire channels in the floor of the kiln.

Figure 7.8(3) shows how to install the final floor layer. The bricks that make up this layer are put on their narrow (75mm, or 3") edges, so that they can more easily bear the loads that are placed on the floor. The bricks are arranged to bridge the fire-channels and leave openings in the floor as shown in (4). The flames can only enter the kiln around the circumference of the firing chamber, which helps to prevent over-firing in the middle of the kiln and under-firing at the edges.

When the floor is completed, the walls of the flues should be smoothed by filling in with clay, sand and shards. This is illustrated in the engineering drawings, but not on these sketches. Curved flue walls make it easier for flames to enter the firing chamber and also help to protect the bricks. Because all the heat entering the chamber must go through the flues, the flues tend to be hotter than any other part of the kiln, including the firebox.

When the kiln is fired it may be necessary to change the heat distribution inside the kiln. This can be achieved by making some of the flue holes larger and some smaller. The original pattern may be less satisfactory where only hardwoods are used as a fuel.

Construction of Flues

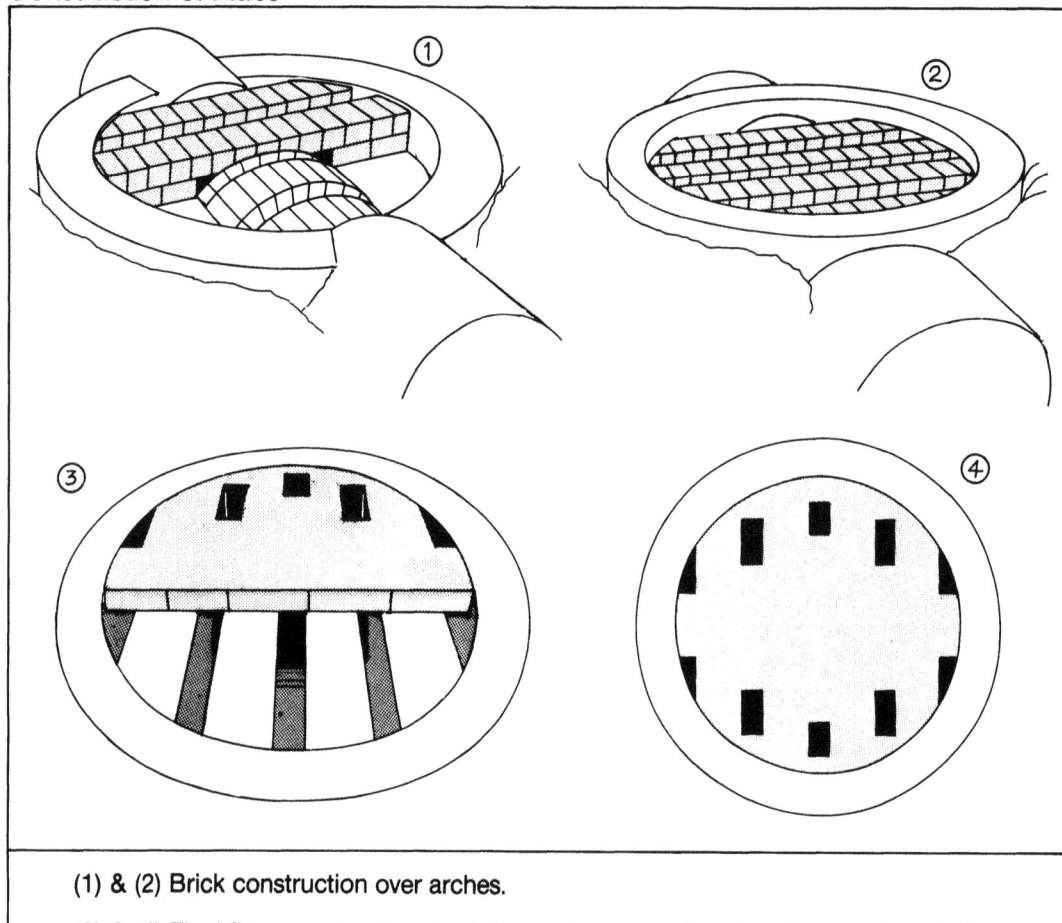

(1) & (2) Brick construction over arches.

(3) & (4) Final floor construction: Bridging arch gaps and leaving flue openings in floor.

Figure 7.8

Wall Construction

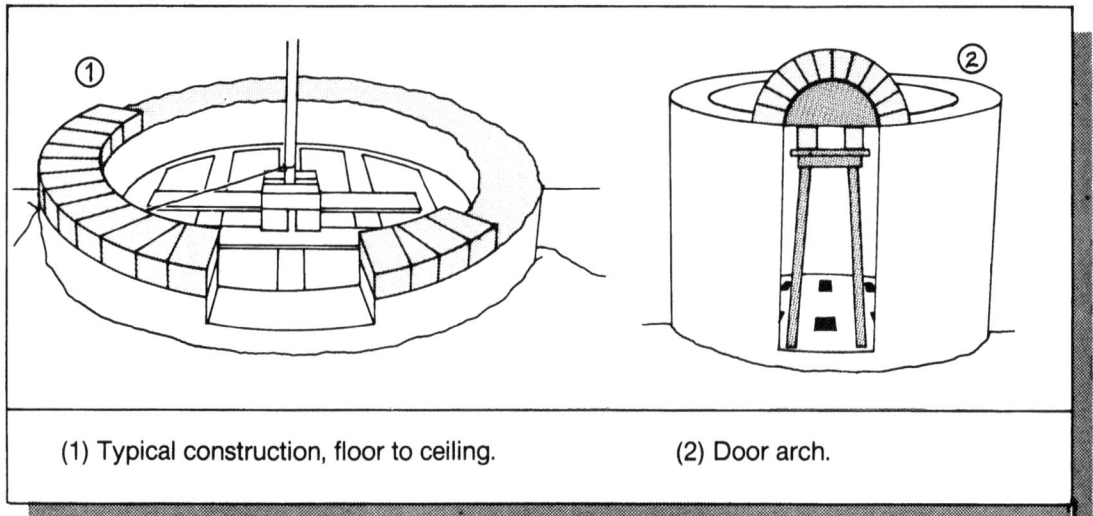

(1) Typical construction, floor to ceiling. (2) Door arch.

Figure 7.9

Generally, the kiln tends to be hottest toward the fireboxes, where the flues abut directly against the walls. Compensate for this by making these holes smaller or by concentrating the fire in the middle of the firebars when stoking. By and large, however, this layout will result in an even spread of temperature.

Wall construction

After the floor is completed, the wall is continued upward, using the wire attached to the pole to ensure the proper curvature. As soon as the floor level is installed, the door opening should be made as shown in Figure 7.9(1). The door must allow an average adult to enter the kiln easily. Once this width is estimated, cut a wooden board to the correct length to ensure a constant width as the door is built. Since most mistakes are made in the construction of the door to the kiln, constant use of the measuring-board and the spirit-level around all three edges of the door jambs is required to ensure acceptable precision.

Figure 7.9(1) also shows a number of bricks stacked around the water pipe used as the centre point for the kiln. As the kiln gets taller, the pipe will flex when the wire is pulled. When the kiln is more than 1m from ground level, these bracing bricks help prevent movement of the pipe. They also ensure that the measuring-wire is kept at the same level as the layer being built. It is a common mistake to use the measuring-wire after its position on the centre pole has slipped down below the level being constructed. This will result in a wall with a smaller diameter. Stacking the bricks around the centre pole to the same height as the wall layer being constructed can help prevent this problem.

Figure 7.9(2) shows the door arch being put in place, supported by a former set on a tall stool. Remember that after the door arch is built, two more layers of bricks still have to be added on top of the arch on the outer skin, and a single layer inside the kiln. The height of the bottom of the door arch is approximately 1.1m above the floor, or about 13 layers of standard English bricks.

Steel Band to Support Dome

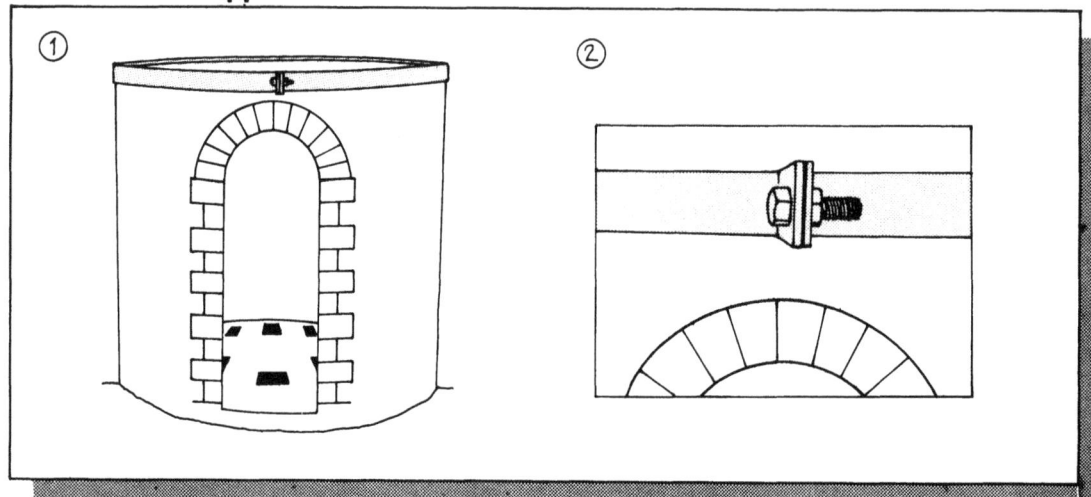

Figure 7.10

Steel band to support dome
Once the wall is built up two layers above the door, the steel band can be installed. For convenience of transport this band is made in three pieces, joined together as shown in Figure 7.10(2). The bolt used here is longer than needed. Therefore, if the band is made in three parts with three bolts having an excess length of 50mm (2") each, it will allow an adjustment of 150mm.

When the band is installed the bolts are done up tight enough to prevent it from slipping down the outer wall, but no tighter. The band should prevent the weight of the roof dome from pushing the walls out, and the tightness of the band will be determined by forces that the kiln applies. Bolting the band tight at this (or any subsequent stage) will create unnecessary tension, and the risk that the wall may be pulled in to a smaller diameter. The bolts must be at least 16mm (⅝") in diameter. There is no point in having a strong metal band if the bolts are thin and weak. The band is placed in such a way as to be 10mm above the top of the outer layer of bricks which are laid parallel to the circumference.

Since there is no inner circle of bricks on the top layer, at this stage, the top of the kiln has a stepped appearance (see Figure 7.11(3).

Setting up for Dome Construction

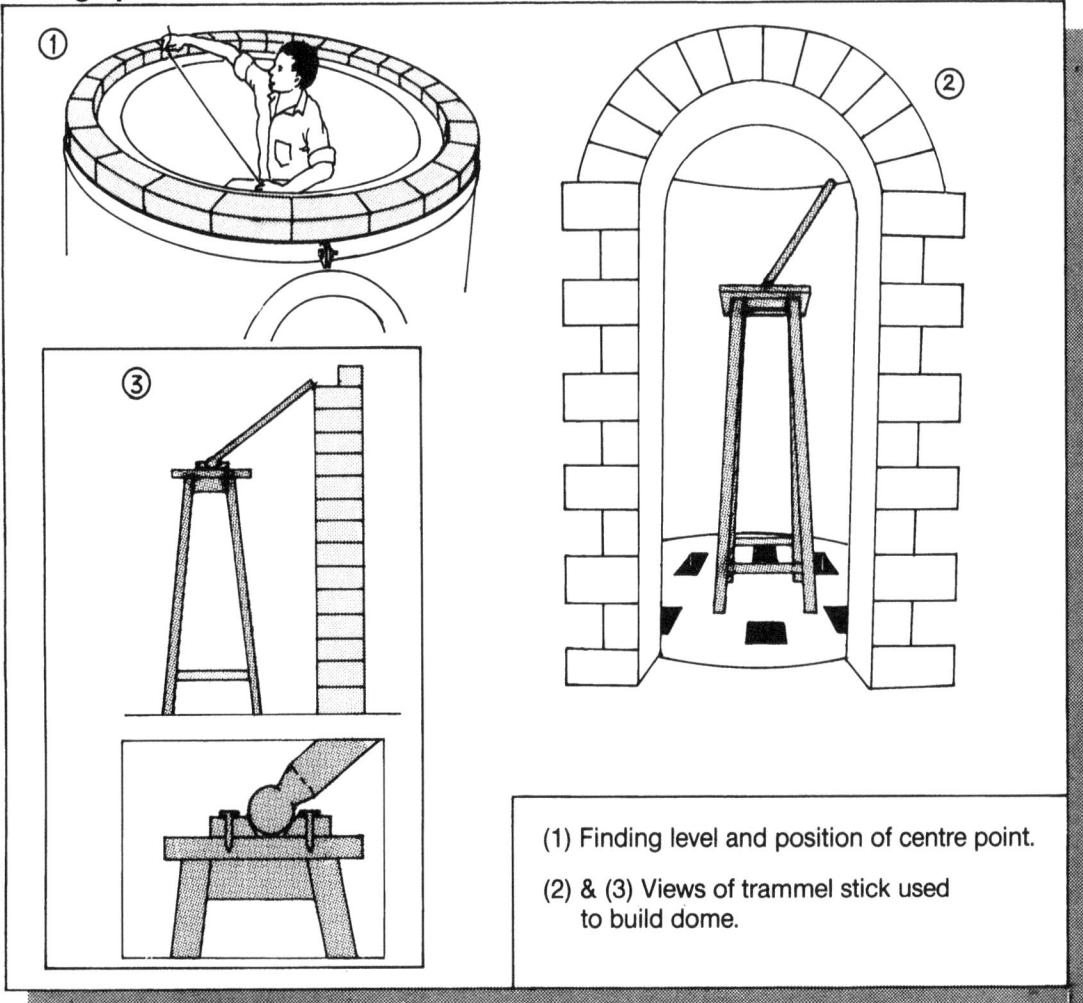

(1) Finding level and position of centre point.

(2) & (3) Views of trammel stick used to build dome.

Figure 7.11

Dome construction

So far, all the arches in the kiln have been constructed using wooden formers to support the weight of the bricks until the arch is complete and able to support itself. On the other hand, a dome can be built without formwork using only a pole that swivels freely in all directions about the centre point of the dome. This pole, known as a trammel stick, is convenient to use on domes up to 5 metres in diameter. Before the stick is used, it is necessary to find the centre point of the planned dome.

Figure 7.11(1) shows how this is done. A string or wooden straight edge is held at the inner edge of the upper row of bricks, and its other end brought down until the string just touches the inner edge of the lower row of bricks. If this is done from both sides of the kiln, the point of intersection is on the level at which the trammel stick must be set. A table or tall stool (2) is set at this height. The drawing shows a stool of exactly the right height, but it may be necessary to either cut the legs of the stool to a shorter length, or elevate it on top of a platform of bricks and wooden wedges.

When the stool is in place, the centre point of the kiln is found again using the string held to the rim. Once the centre point is marked, a piece of wood with a tapered hole is nailed to the stool with the hole set over the centre mark. The hole should have a diameter 30mm at the top and 20mm at the bottom.

A broomstick with a diameter of about 30mm is then carved to have a ball at one end (Figure 7.11(3), lower illustration). This ball enables the stick to freely rotate, while maintaining a constant length. The stick is then cut to the exact length necessary to rest on the inner edge of the lower rim of bricks that form the rim of the kiln (Figure 7.11(3), upper illustration).

Check to be sure that the stick touches the rim at the same length all the way around the kiln before it is cut to length. If it does not touch the rim uniformly, then the centre has not been properly established.

When the stick rests correctly around the entire circumference, the stool is firmly positioned. Bracing struts of wood are nailed to the legs of the stool and wedged to the kiln walls. These are not shown in the drawings.

Be careful to set the trammel stick in a proper position, on a base that is rigid and firm.

When constructing the dome, the mason needs very high quality bricks and a steady supply of mortar. Figure 7.12(2) shows how the bricks are laid on a thick bed of mortar and tapped into place with a cooper's hammer, with their lower end resting on the trammel stick.

Figure 7.12(3) and (4) show how bricks are laid using the stick. Notice that the centre line of the brick, in both planes, is also in line with the centre line of the trammel stick.

A lot of mortar is needed to establish the proper angle of the bricks in a dome. If

Dome Construction

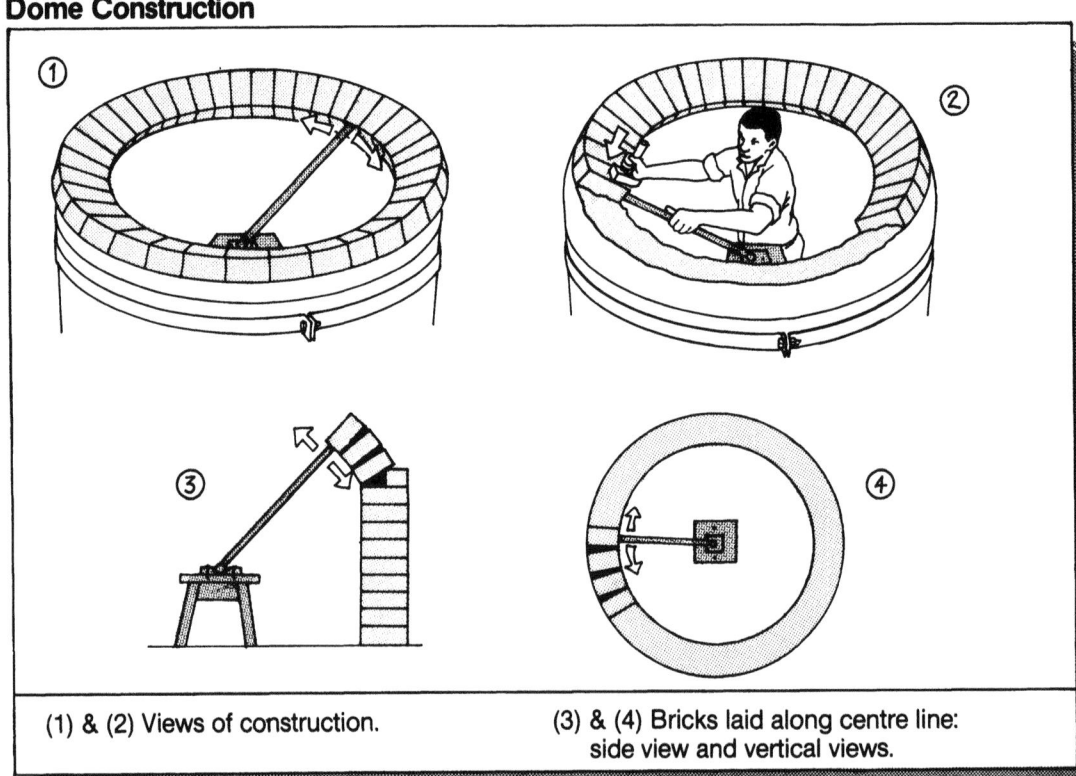

(1) & (2) Views of construction.

(3) & (4) Bricks laid along centre line: side view and vertical views.

Figure 7.12

Chimney Construction

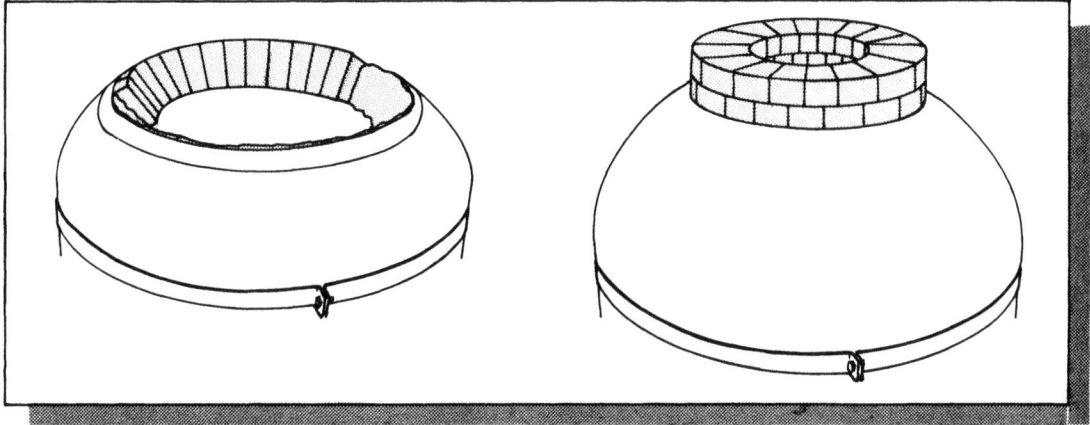

Figure 7.13

there is too much or too little mortar, the angle will be wrong. The most common mistake in building a dome is to use too much mortar. This does not cause problems in the first few layers, but as the dome climbs more towards the vertical the bricks will become vertical, or even go past the vertical. When that happens there is nothing to stop them from falling into the kiln.

The basic rules are:

○ make sure that the bottom, inner edges of the brick are in contact with the row of bricks underneath; and
○ make sure that the centre line of the brick lines up with the trammel stick, both when viewed from the side (Figure 7.12(3), and from above (Figure 7.12(4).

When the ring of bricks is complete it will be very strong. If a brick moves inward, it will only be driven more tightly against its neighbours. Once a brick is put in place it is tapped against the trammel stick in line with the centre of the dome and then firmly against its neighbour on the bottom edge. This will prevent the neighbouring brick from falling in. If the clay mortar is of the proper consistency the bricks should not shift. It is best to make the mortar slightly stiffer than usual to stop the bricks from sliding.

Once the ring of bricks is completed, the trammel stick should be swung around the entire layer to make sure that no bricks have crept inward. Before building the next layer, shards and stiff clay should be hammered into the gaps between the bricks. This will ensure that the bricks are locked into place.

Chimney construction

Using the method described under dome construction, the dome should be built until a centre hole not less than 38cm (15") and not more than 45cm (18") in diameter remains to form the chimney outlet.

The outlet is made from two rings of bricks, laid radially as shown in Figure 7.13(1). Tapered bricks are shown but standard bricks can be used, as long as the gaps are properly filled with clay and shards.

The hole at the centre is the same diameter as the hole at the lower edge of the dome. As a result the chimney rings will overhang the upper edge of the dome opening. This gap is filled in with a mixture of stiff mortar to make a smooth tubular chimney opening (See drawing no. 1.6, p. 93). To make sure that the chimney opening is circular try to use a washing bowl, of a similar diameter to the lower opening in the dome, as a former. When the chimney has been completed, the entire dome is plastered in mortar to seal any gaps that may exist and provide buttressing to the two rows of chimney bricks.

Afterword

Although we have tried to make this manual as complete as possible, we realize that manuals are only one tool for establishing a successful business. Sound management, appropriate technology, careful attention to detail, hiring and training competent employees, and the ability to market the product(s) are essential in bolstering a business's chances of success.

We wish you the best of luck in your efforts. If you have a problem with any of this material, either contact ATI Jikos or CARE. Just as important, if you find a better way of doing something, or you have any tips you would like to share with us or other entrepreneurs, write to us. Ultimately we hope to put out a semi-annual newsletter to keep all of us involved in this environmental venture informed about the state of the art in ceramic-lined jikos.

The Completed Kiln

Figure 7.14

Appendix A
Use and care of the jiko

1. Load the stove with charcoal that already has been broken down to a convenient size. The airgate should be open.
2. Do not break up large pieces of the charcoal inside the stove.
3. Use a mixture of ash and kerosene underneath the stove to light it.
4. Fan the fire after lighting, again with the airgate open.
5. Leave the airgate open if a lot of heat is needed quickly.
6. Close the airgate for slow cooking.
7. Do not pour water on the stove to extinguish the fire.
8. and 9 This is the correct way to extinguish the fire: first, shake the ashes and coals out on to the ground; then pour water on the coals.

Appendix B
Engineering Drawing Set

The drawings of the jigger-jolley moulding machine (pp. 75–92) will enable a competent technician to manufacture the machine in no more than ten days. These drawings show the machine from two different perspective views, which helps to illustrate the layout. A special perspective shows only the drive train from the motor, through the counter–shaft, to the wheelhead and mould. The machine is then shown 'exploded' to provide an idea how to assemble the component parts, and also in orthogonal projection: plan view, side elevation and end elevation. The various parts of the machine are numbered on the exploded view (excluding bearings and the motor). These numbers correspond to the drawings that follow, in which each component is drawn independently in orthogonal projection.

The drawings of the kiln (pp. 92–98) show orthogonal projection and sections through it at various positions. Two sections are shown in perspective views, illustrating the arrangement of the flues and the arches that support the floor of the kiln.

Jigger-Jolley Moulding Machine

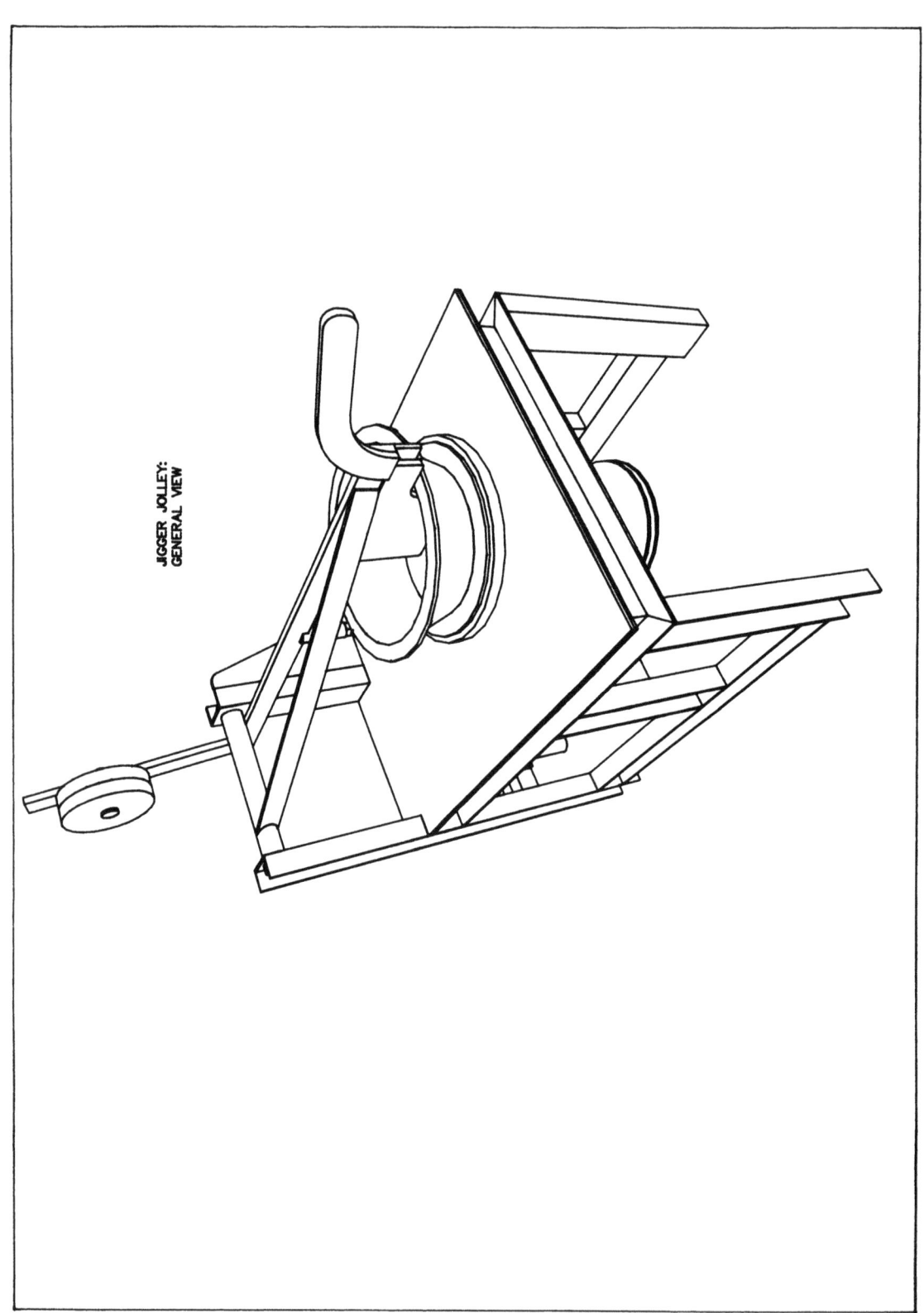

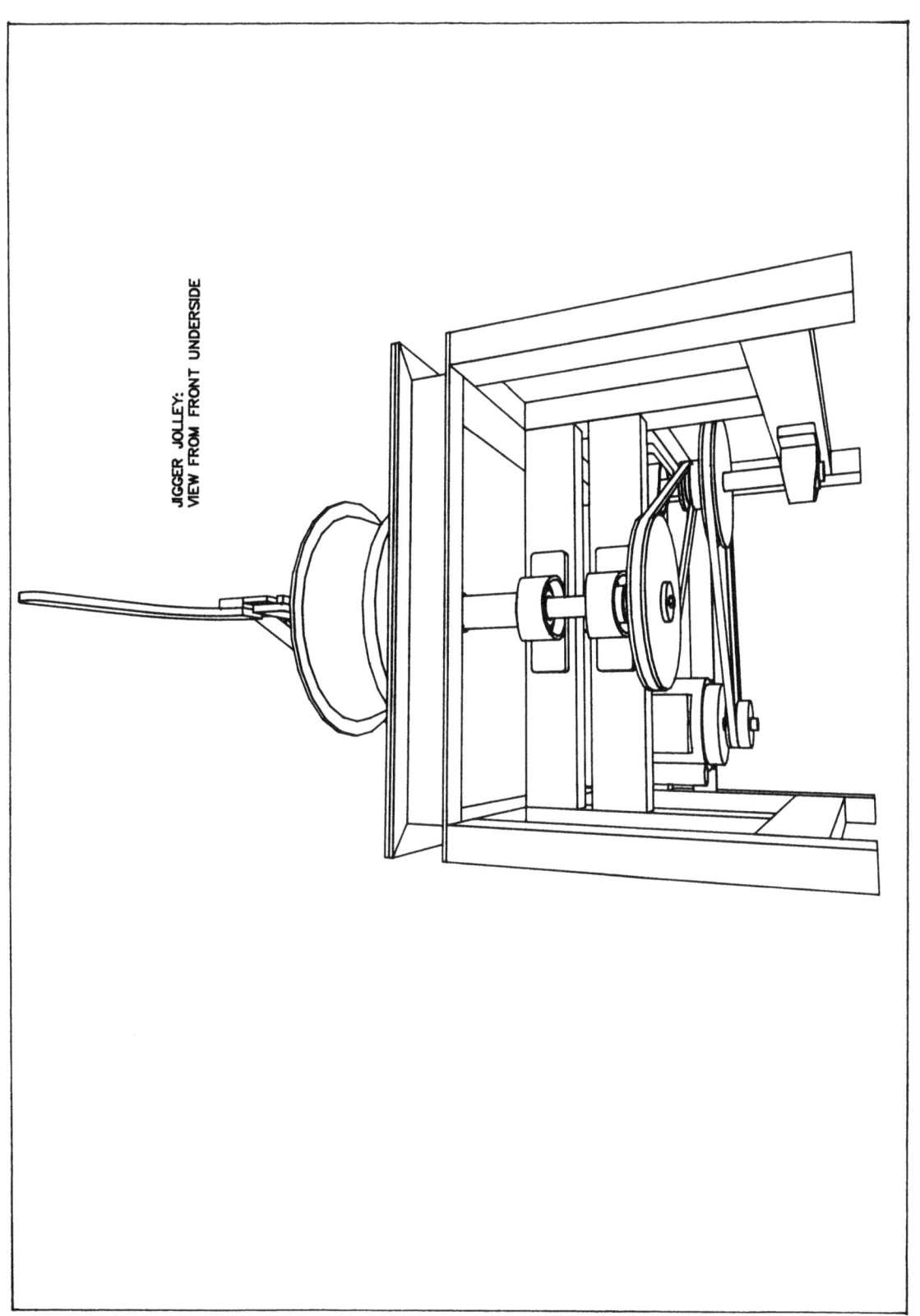

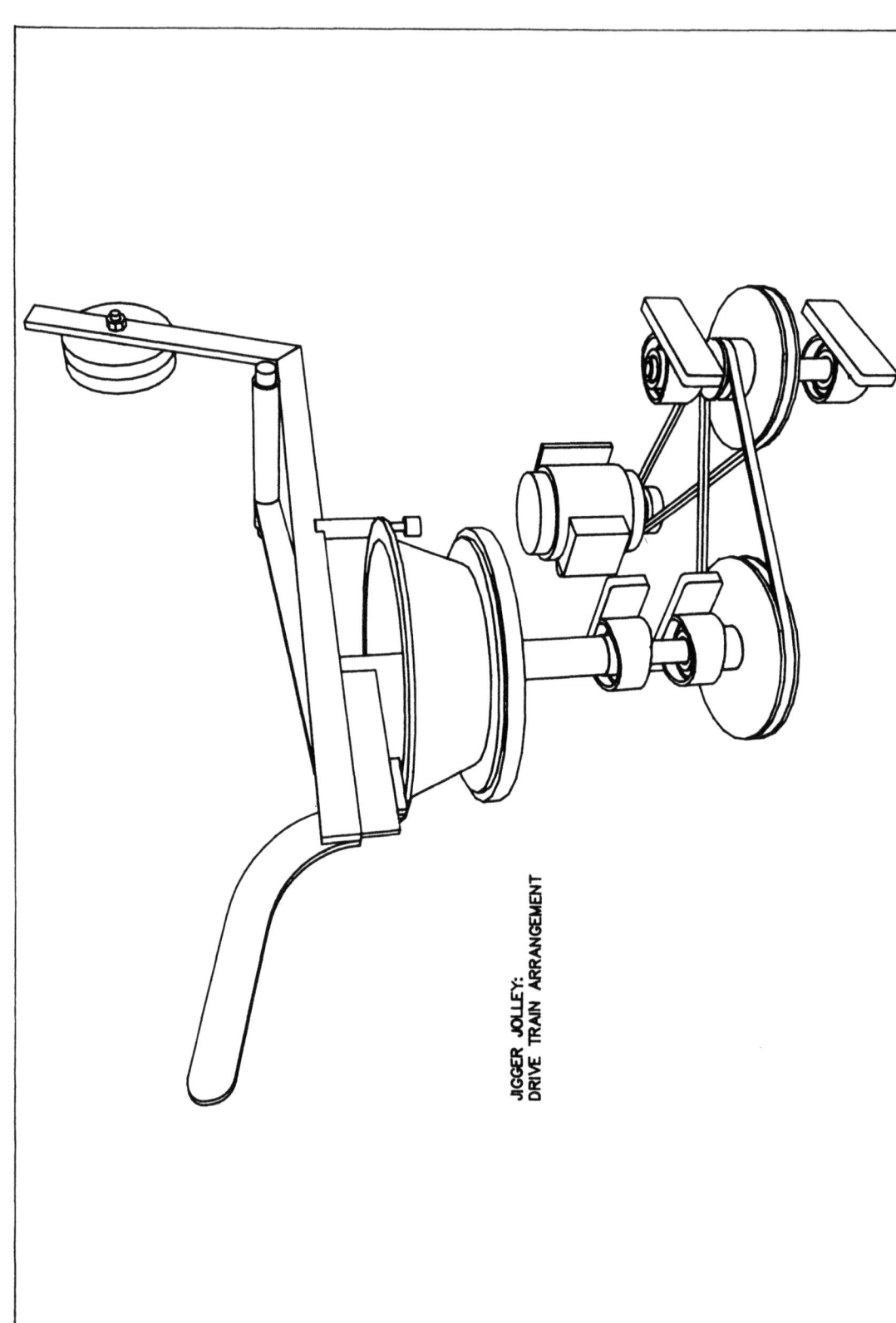

JIGGER JOLLEY:
DRIVE TRAIN ARRANGEMENT

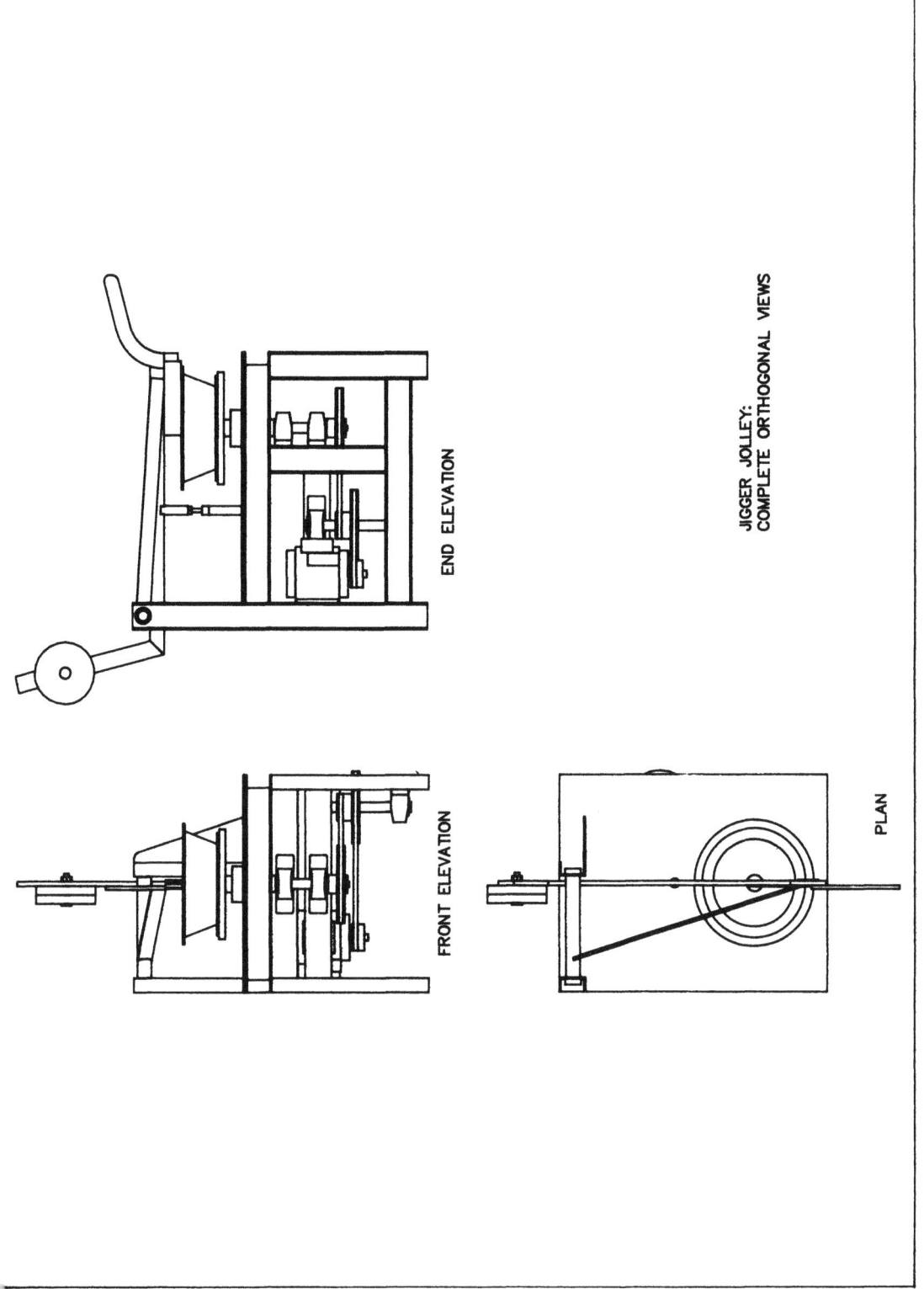

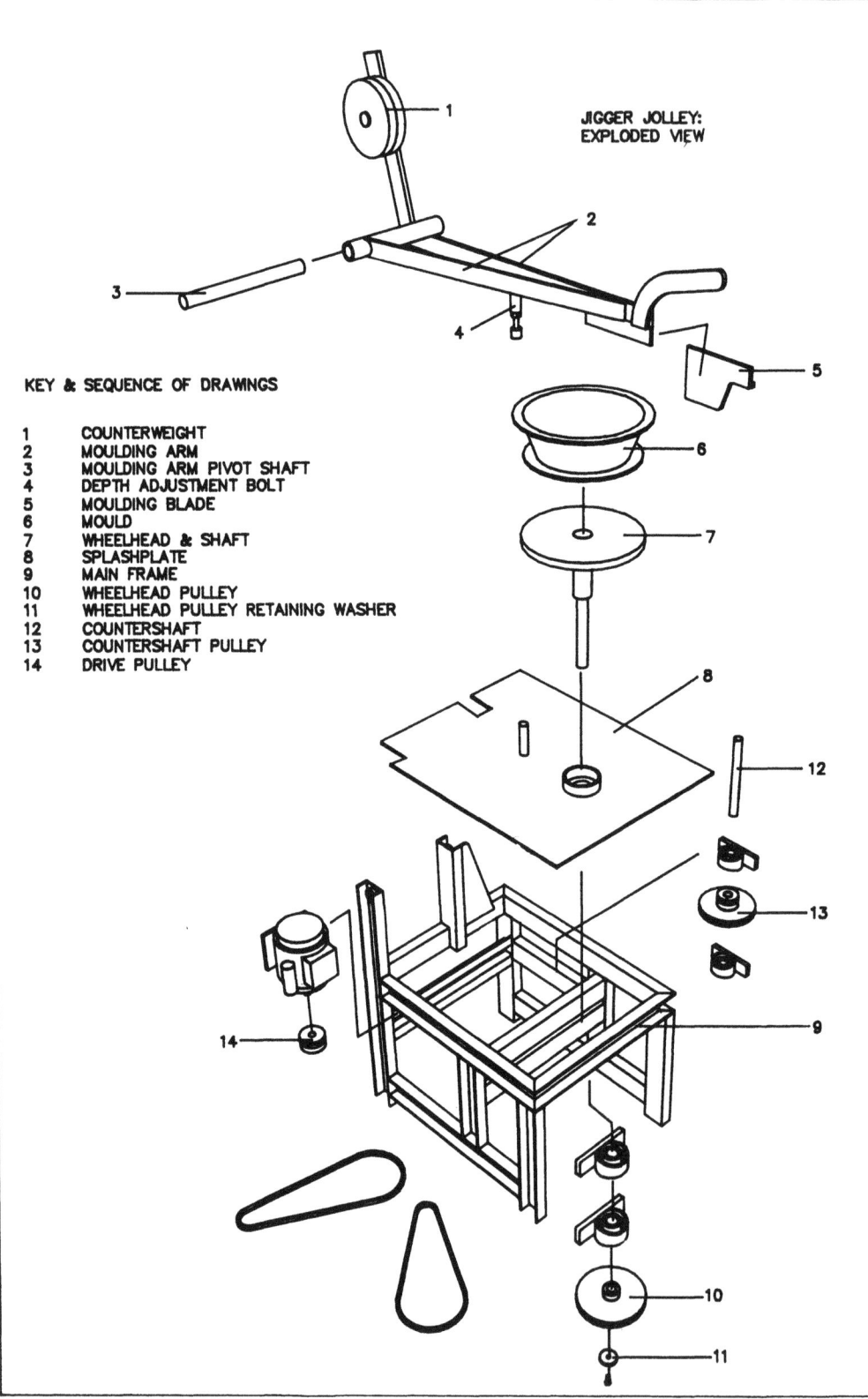

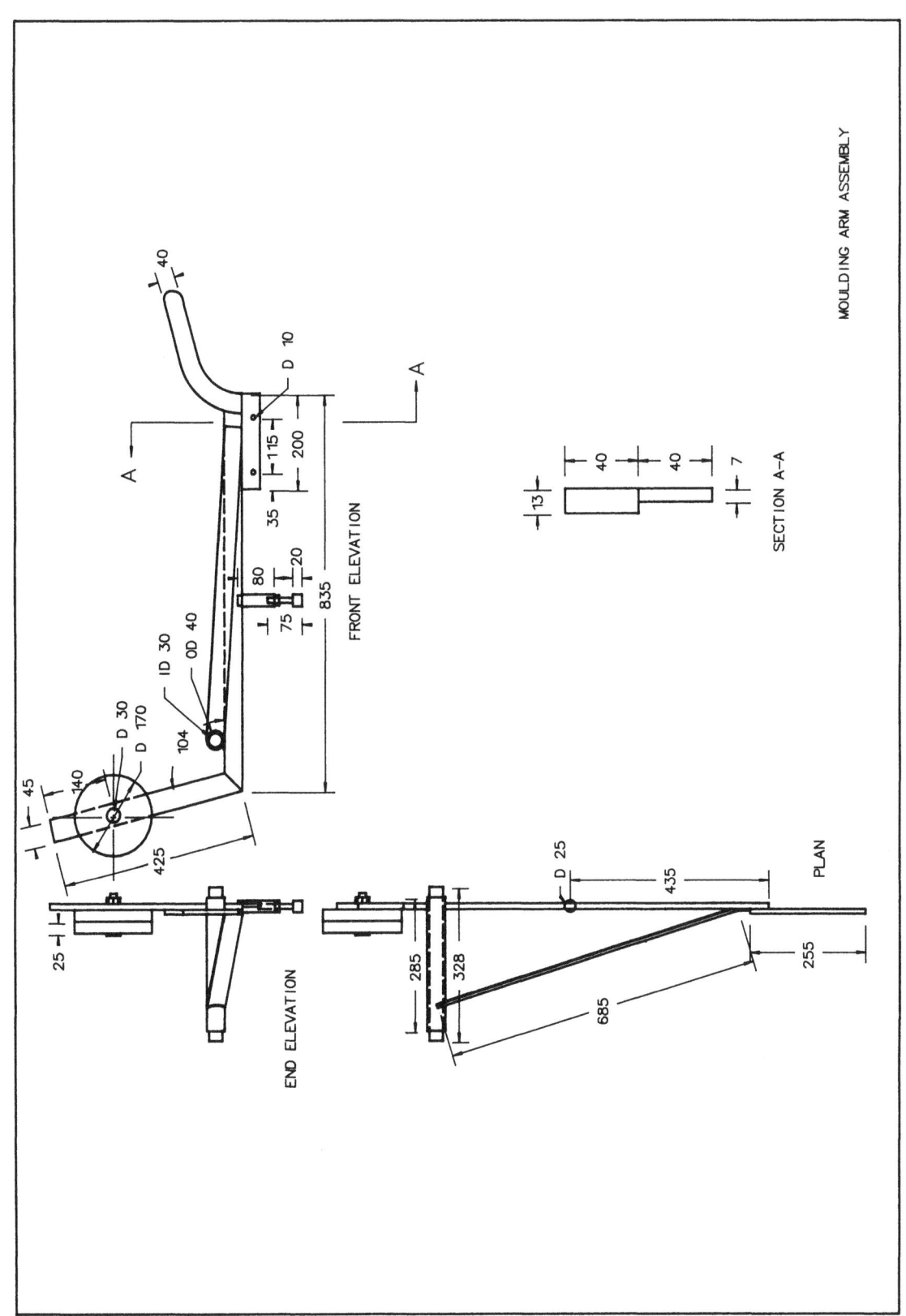

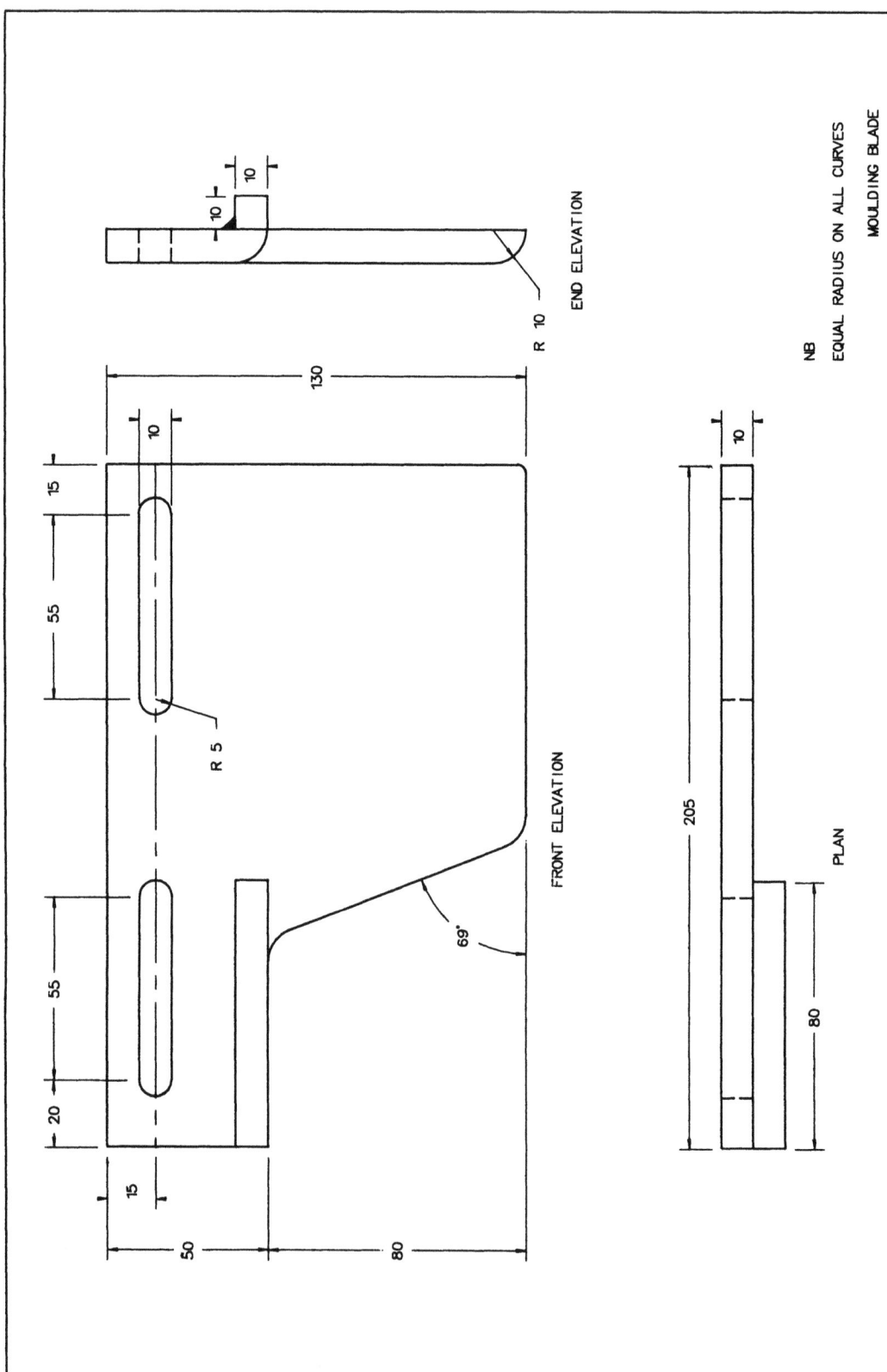

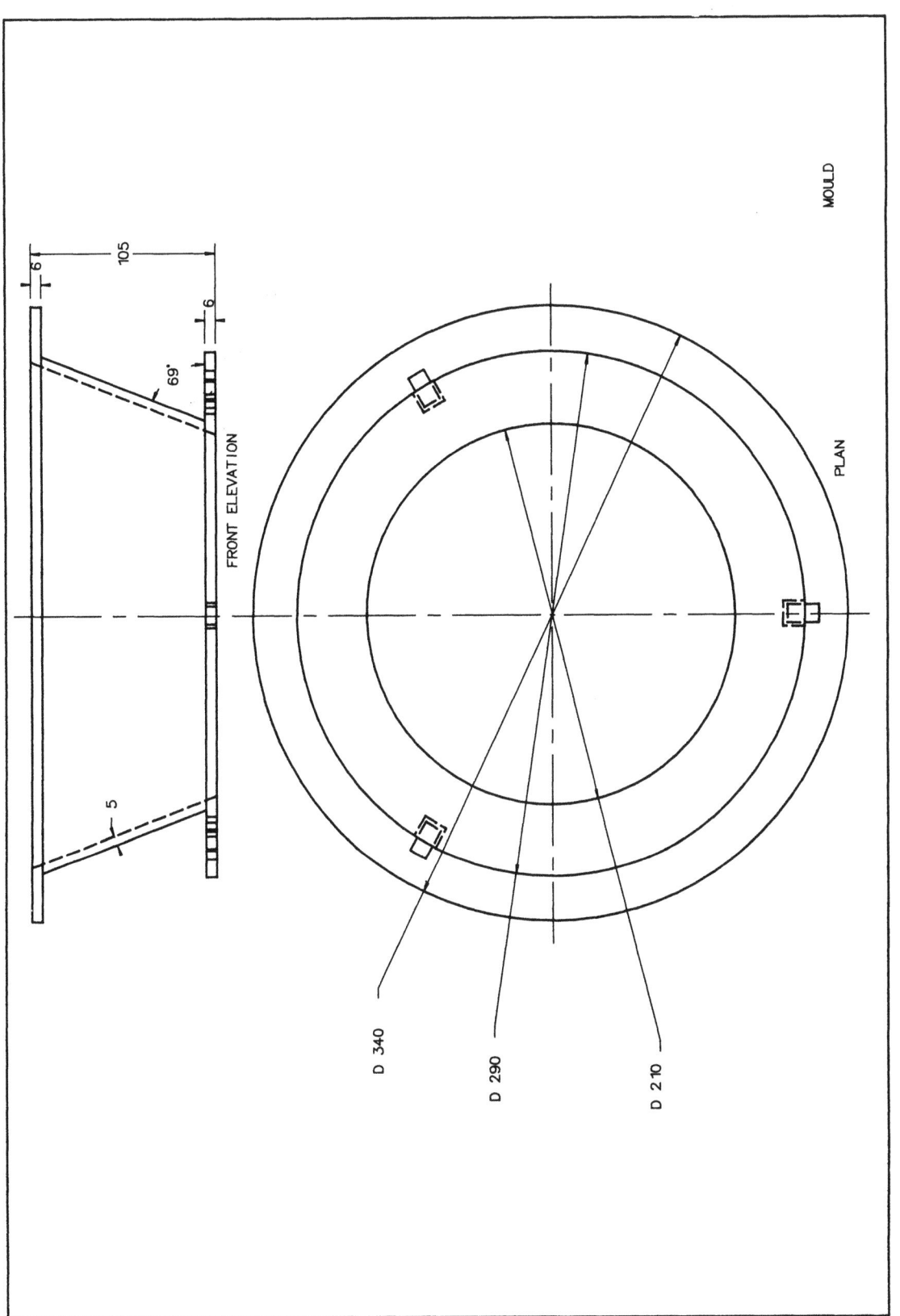

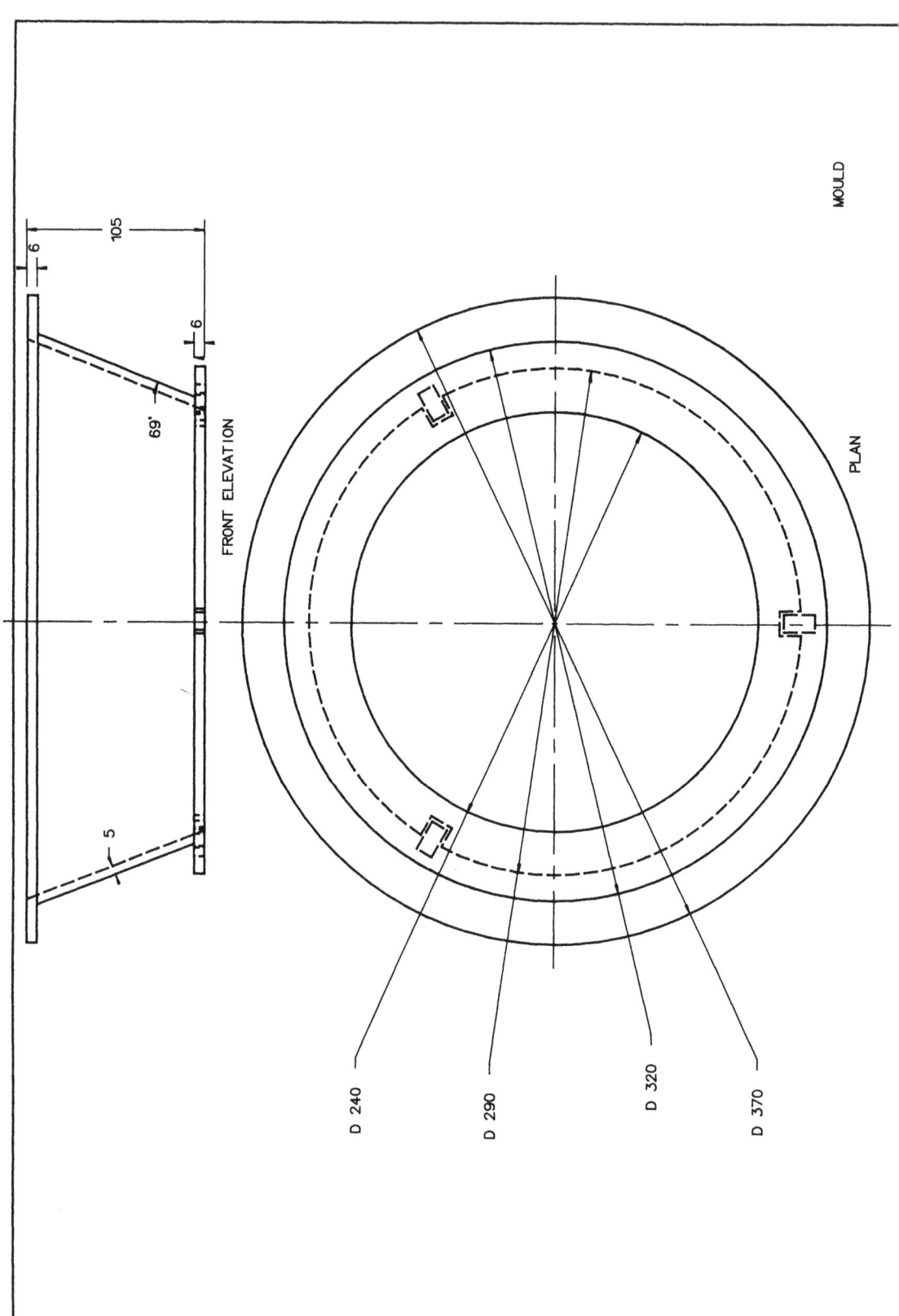

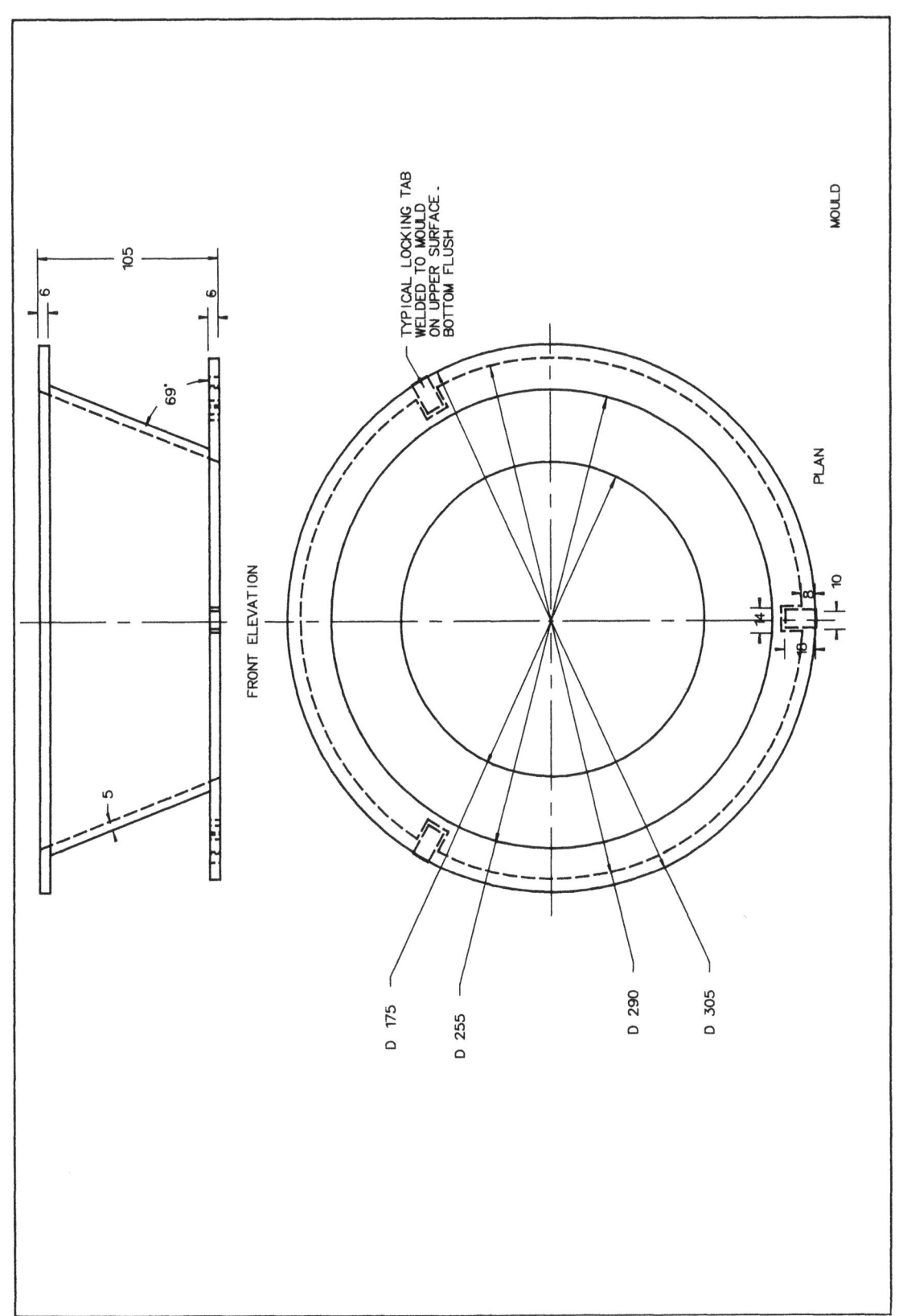

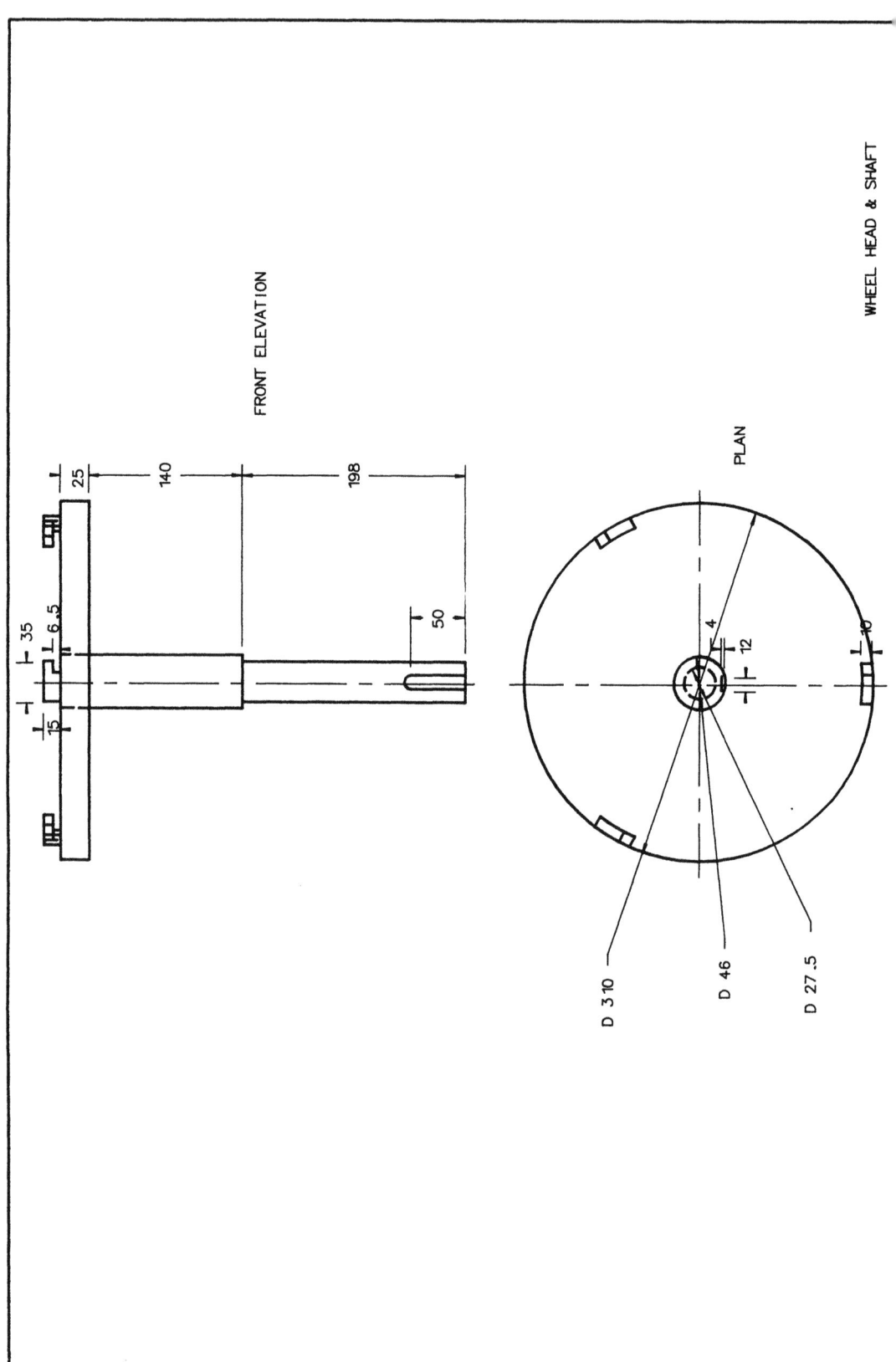

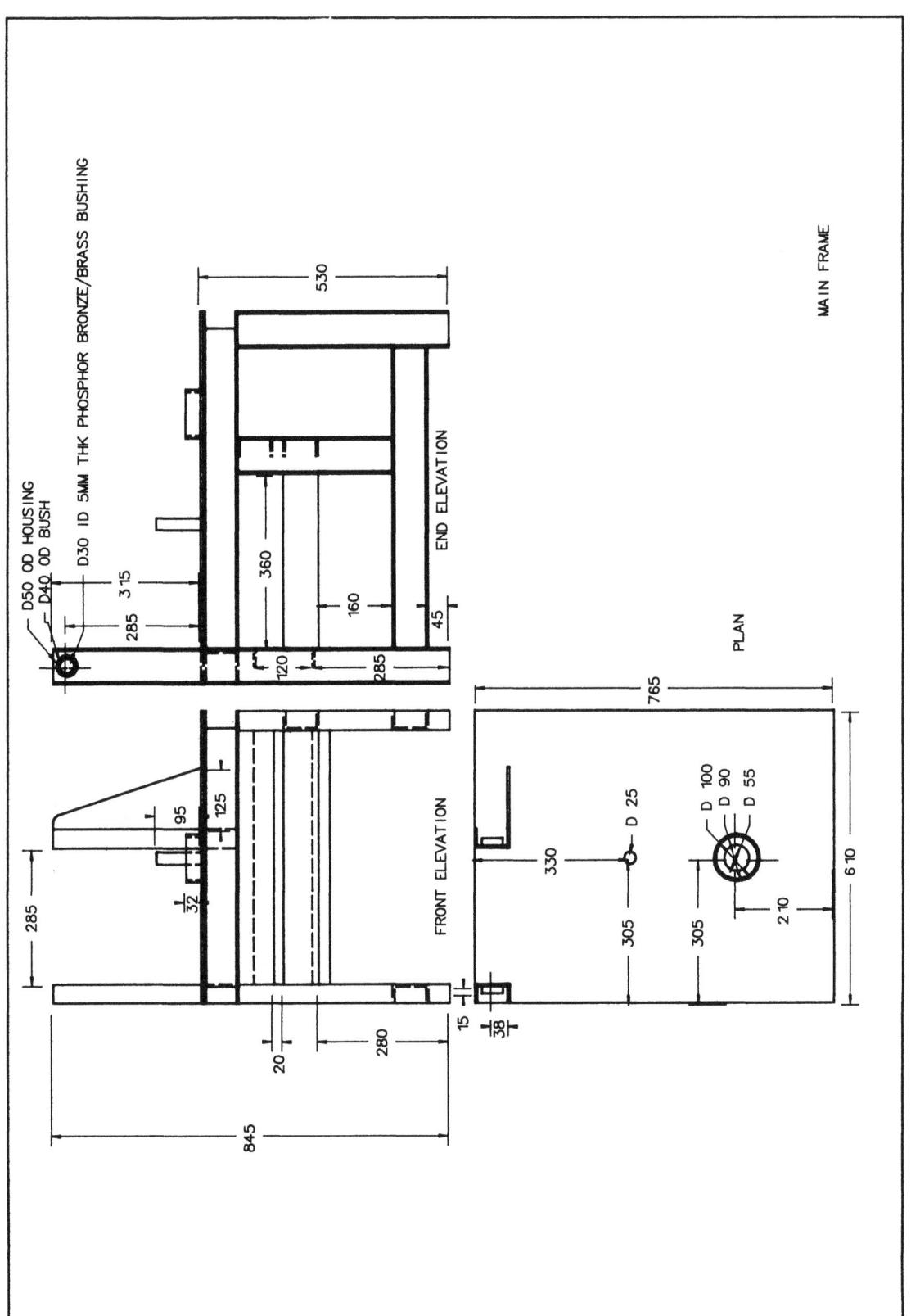

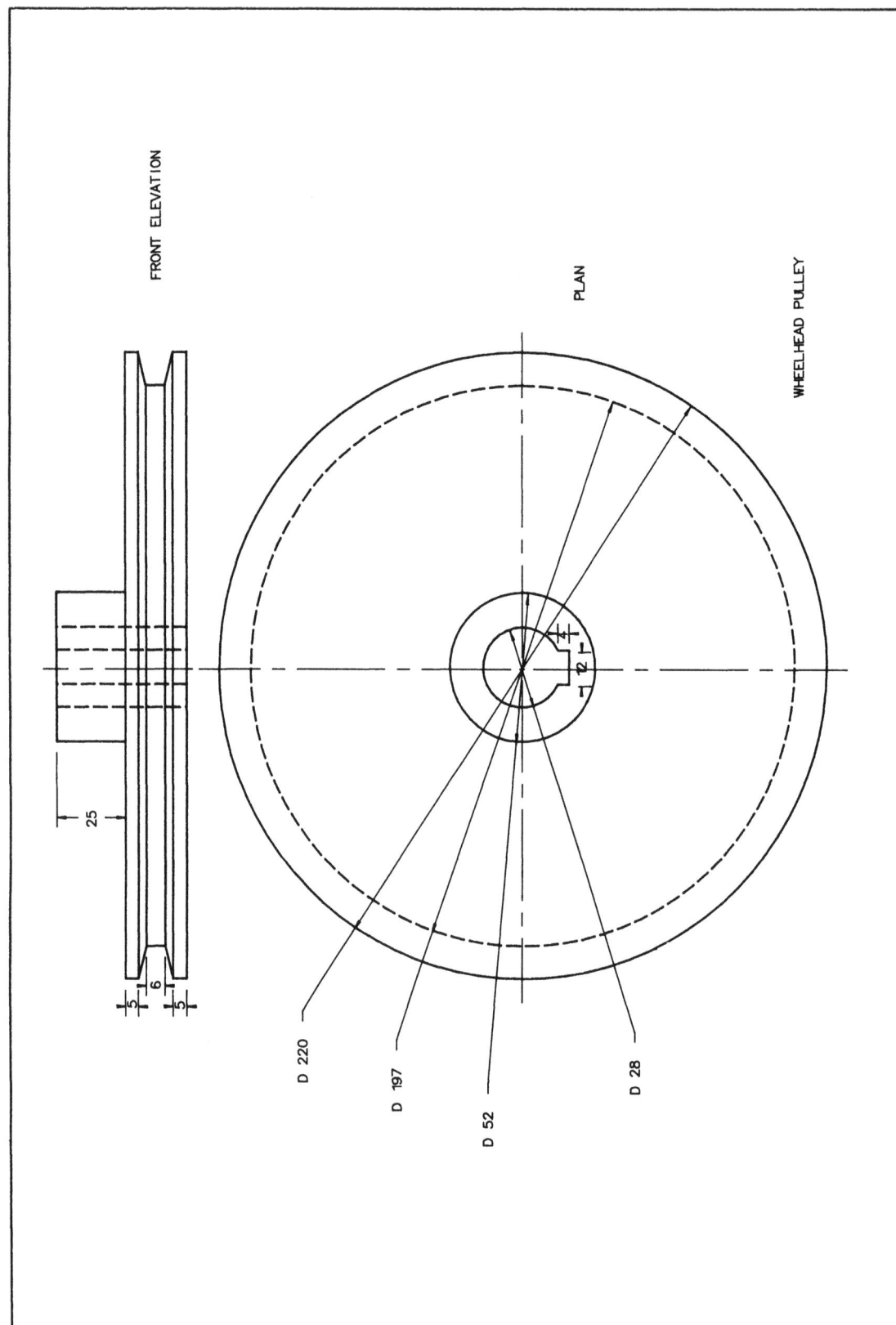

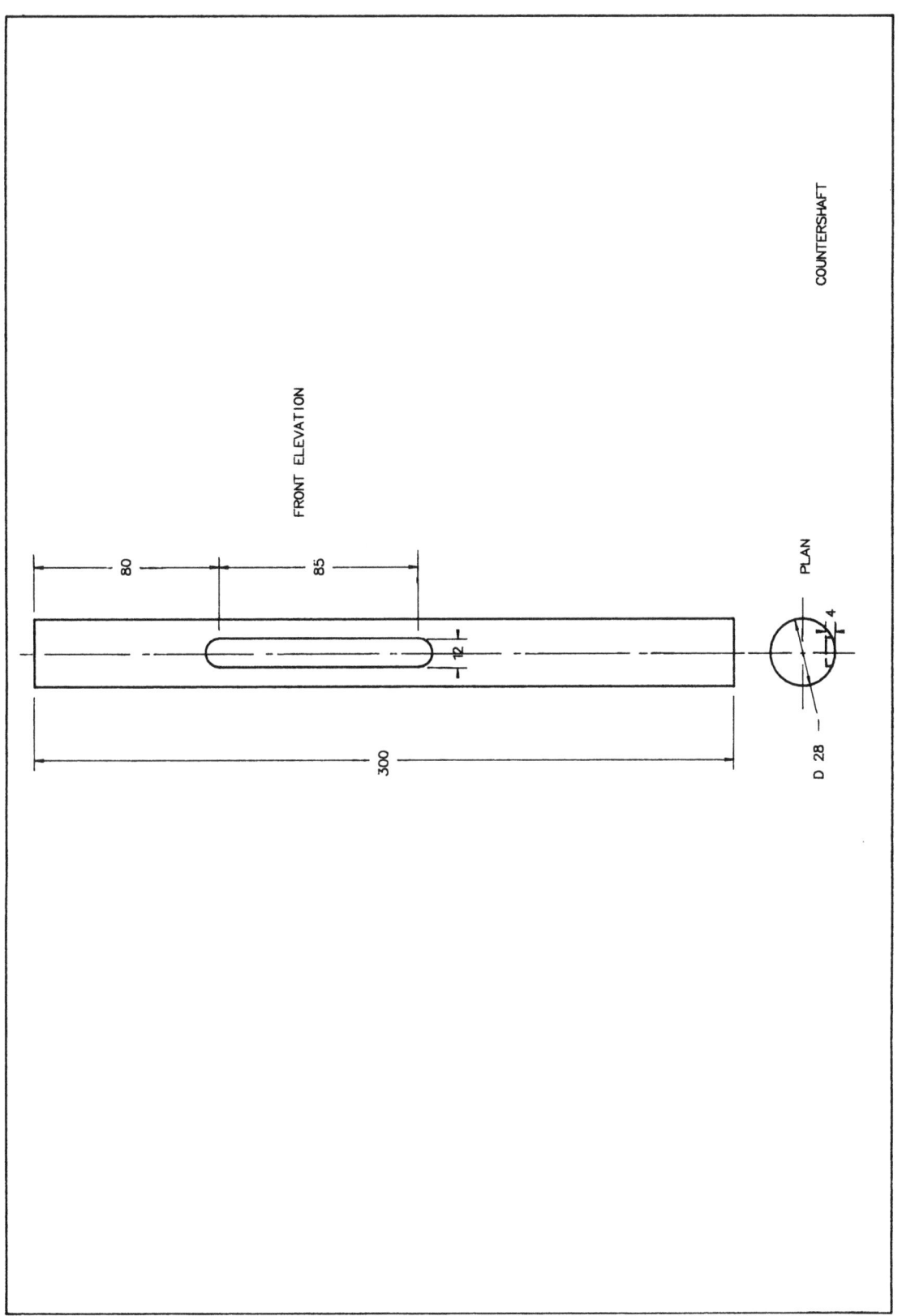

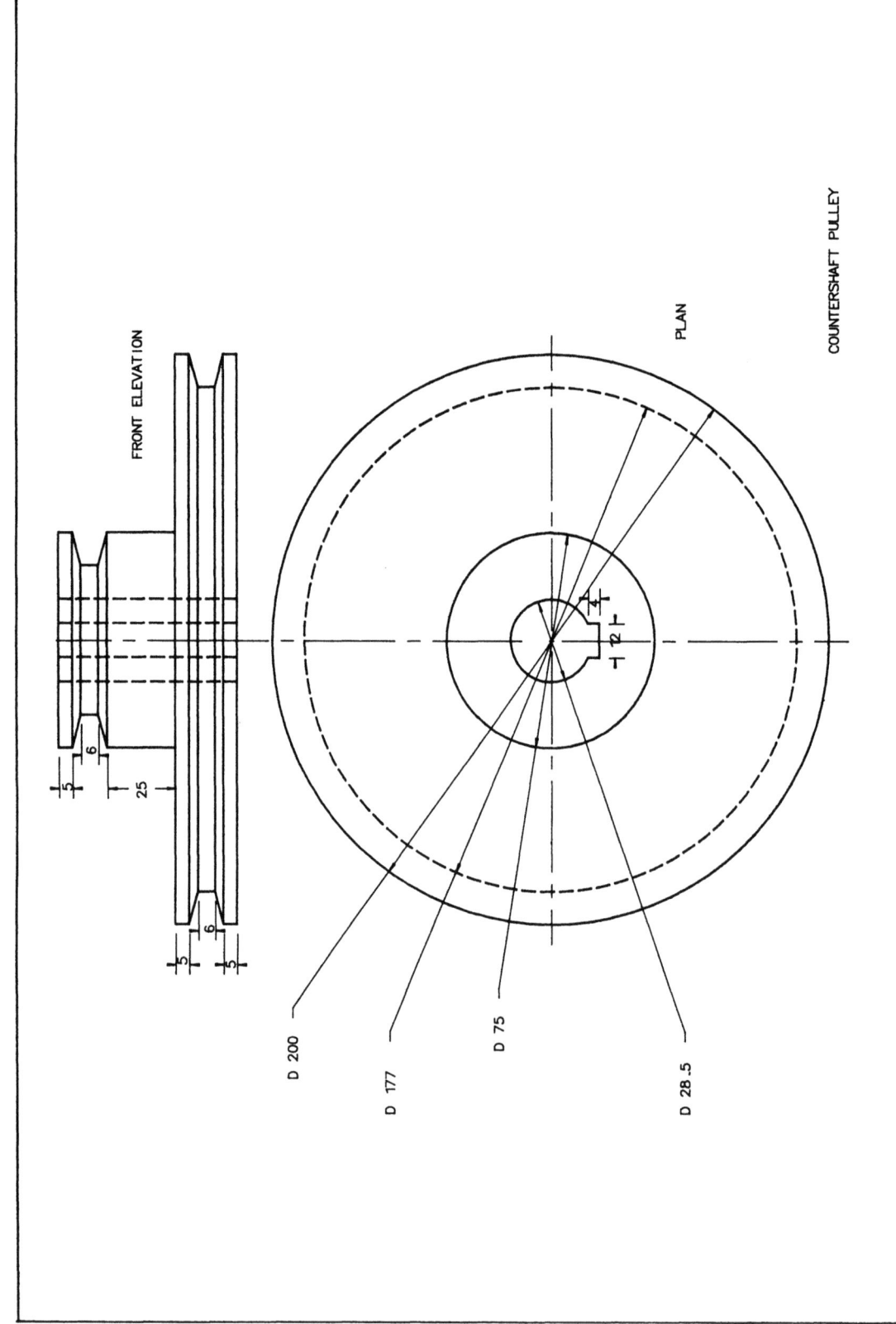

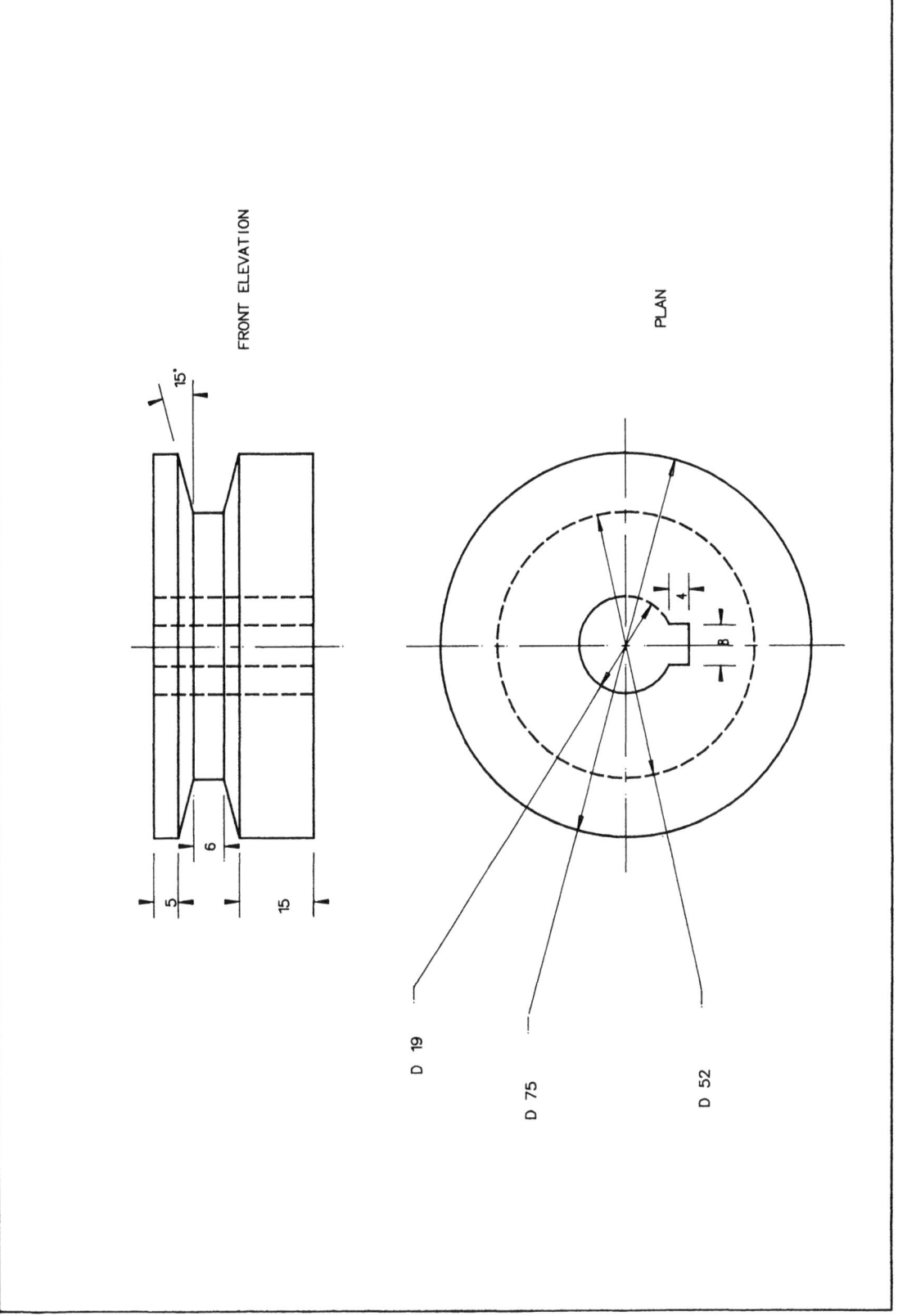

Kiln

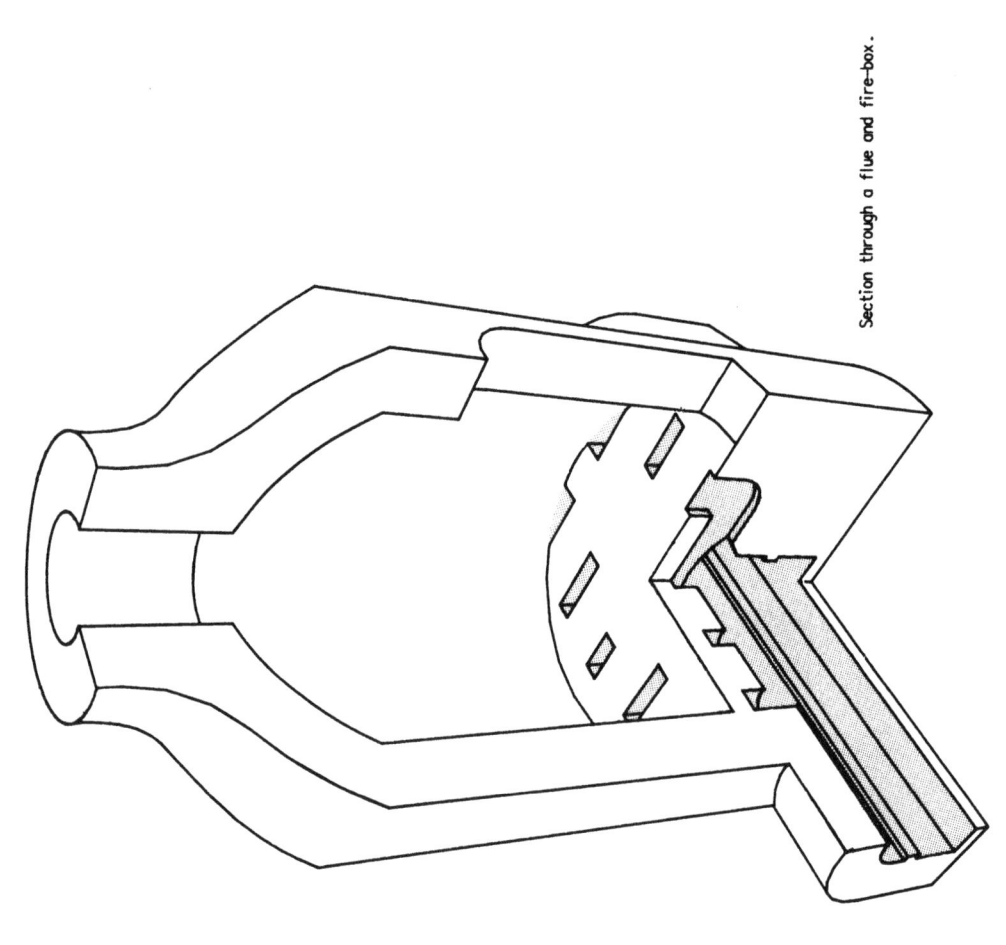

Section through a flue and fire-box.

TIGONI KILN
DWG No ⊥ 1

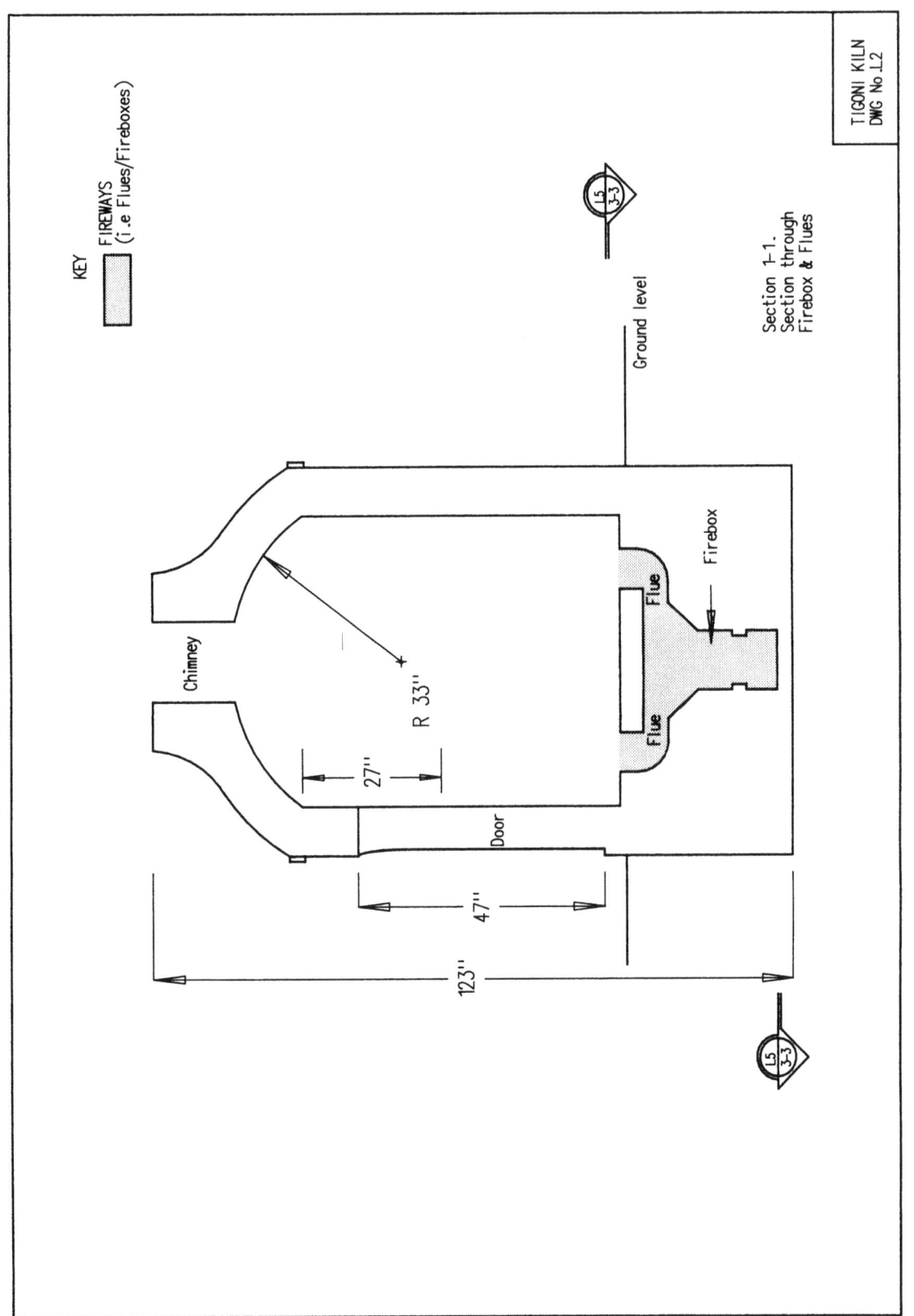

Section through floor arch and the fire-box.

TIGONI KILN

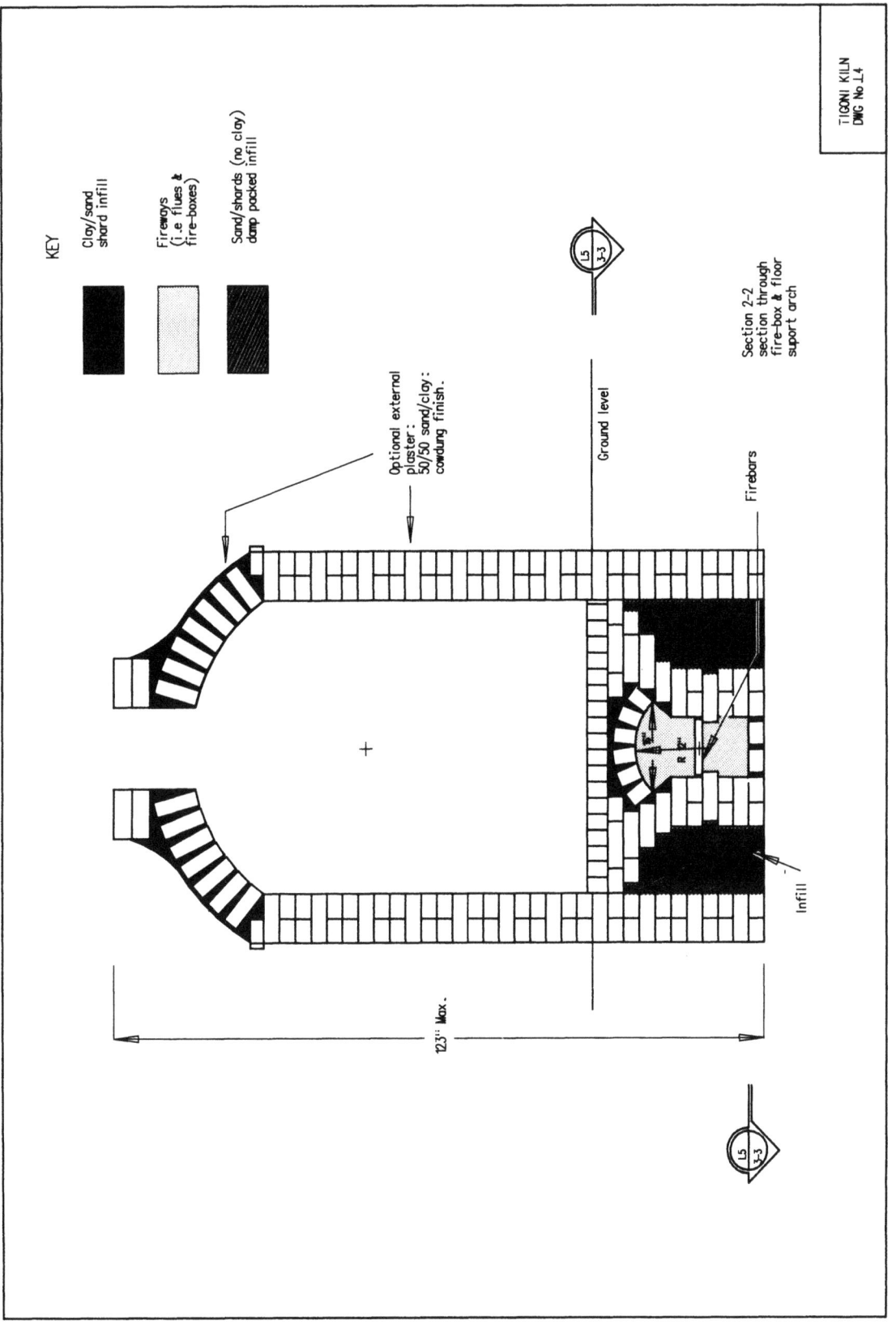

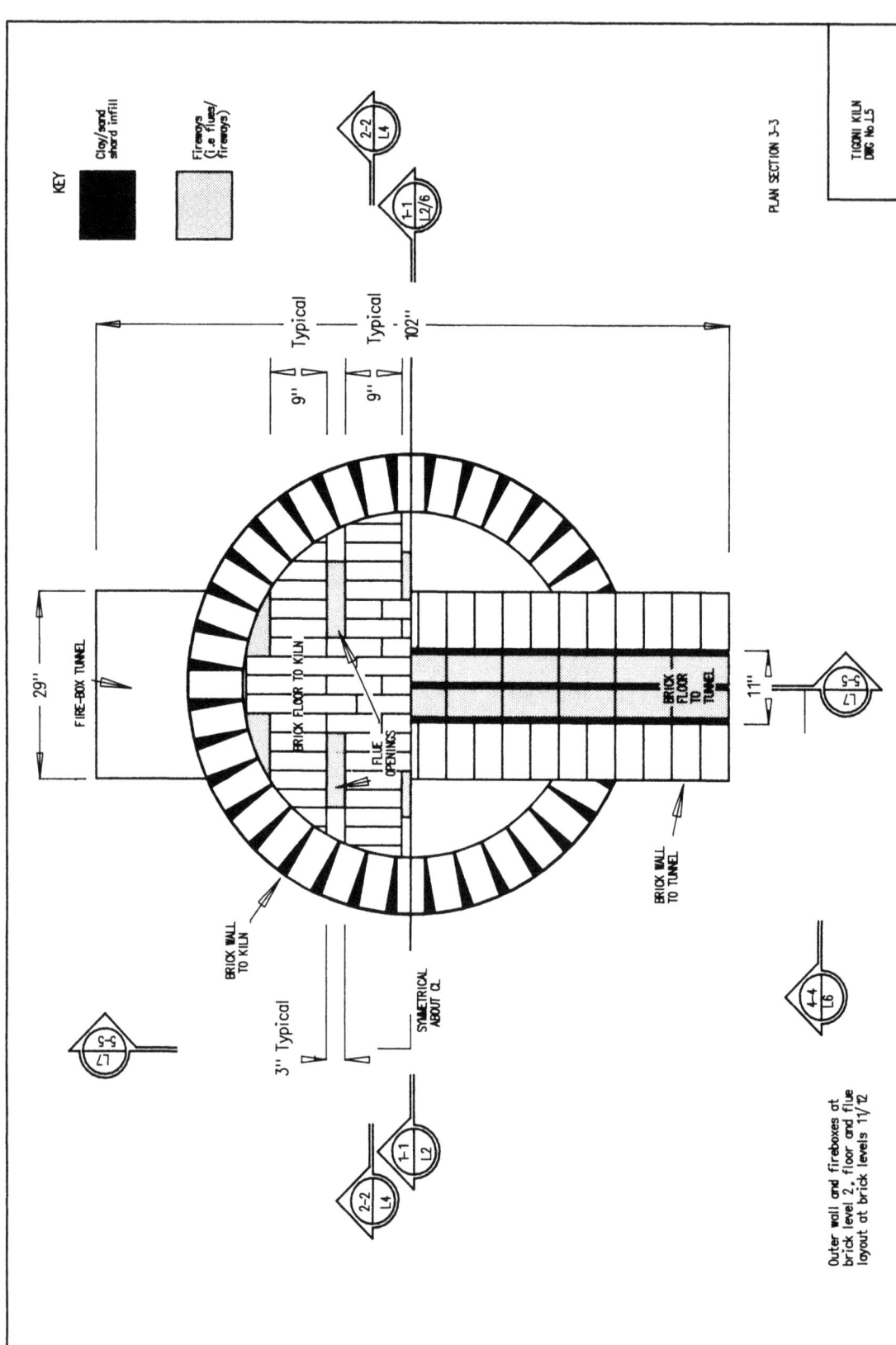

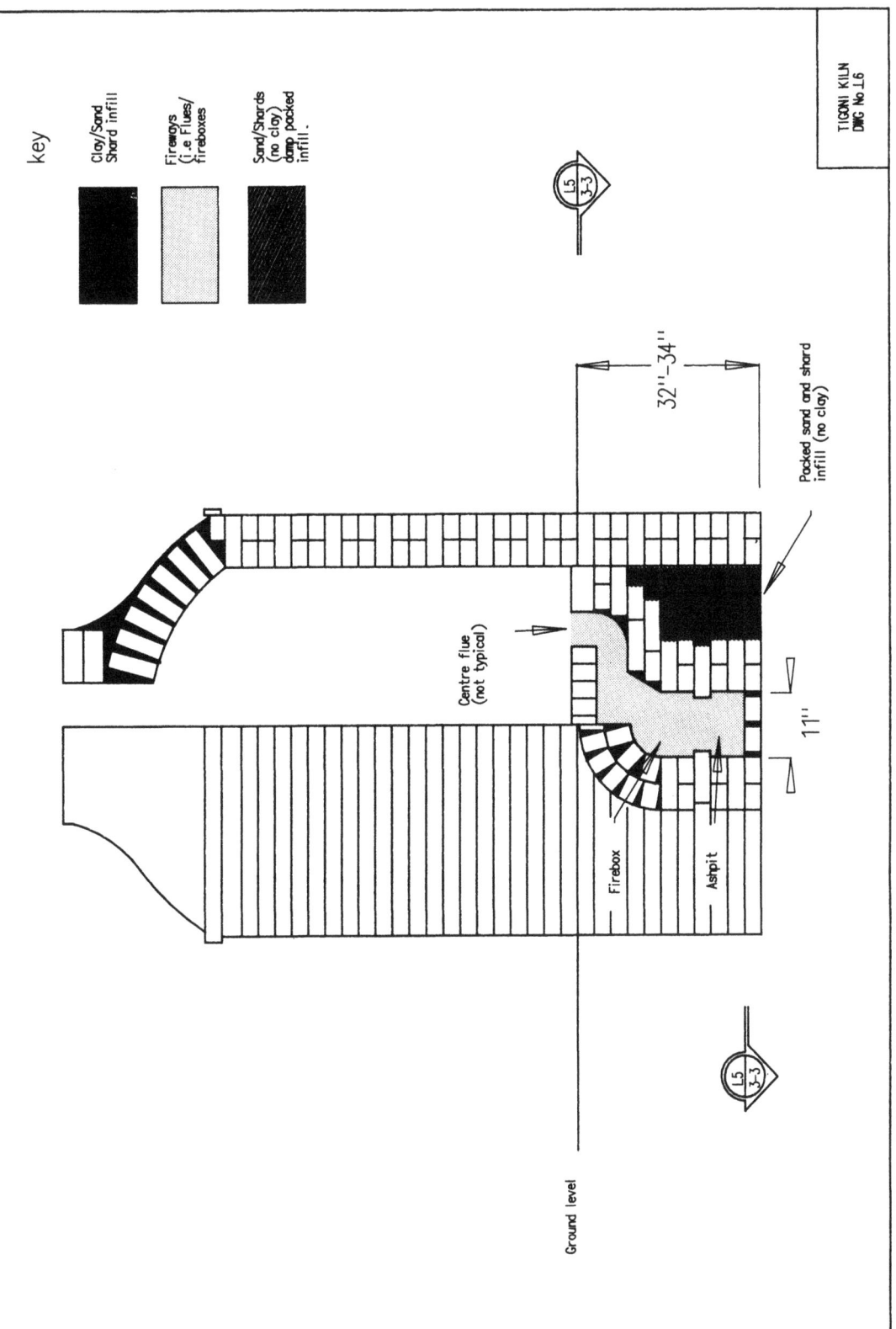

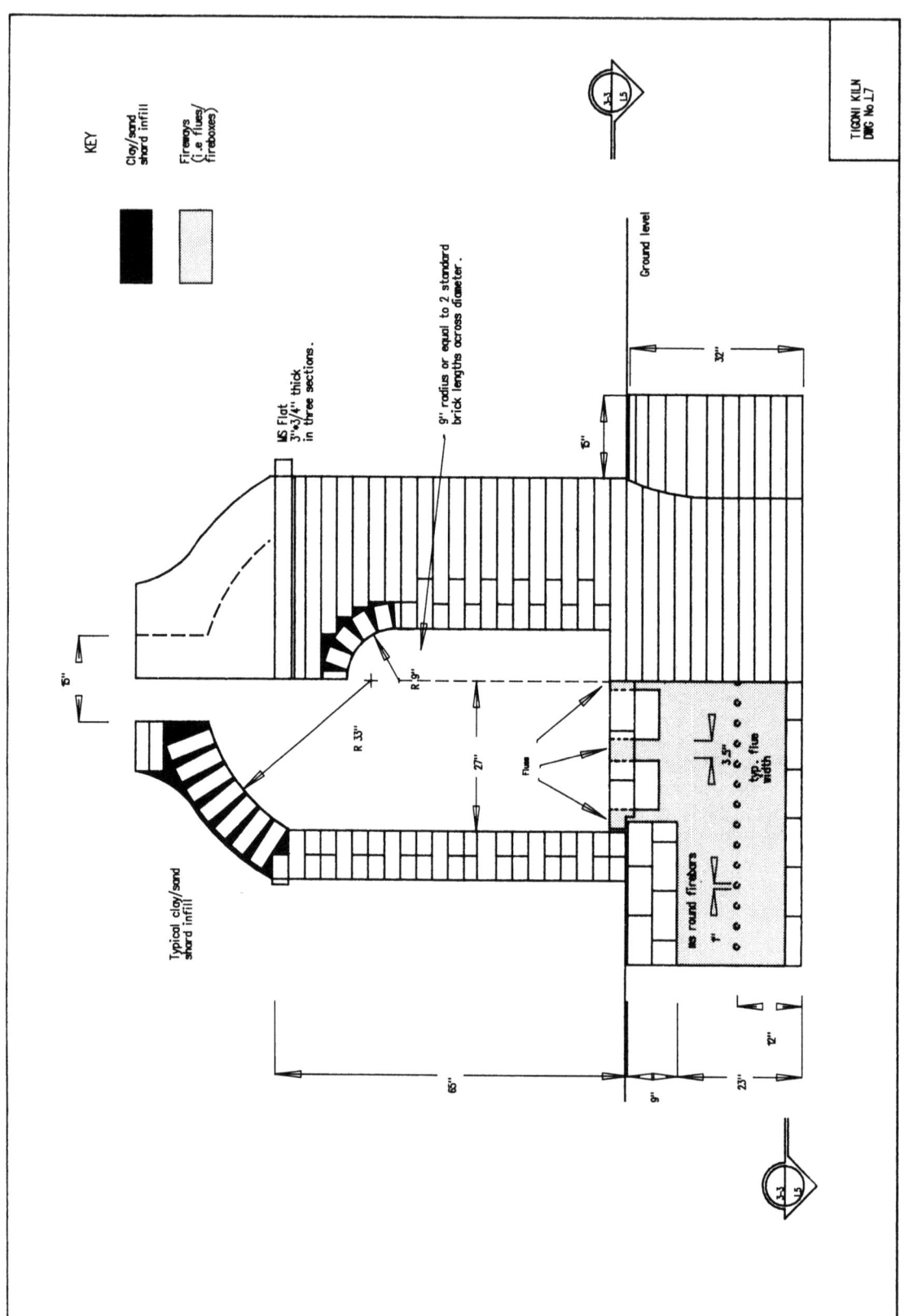

Appendix C
Useful addresses

Clay mixers

Soldner Pottery Equipment Inc.,
PO Box 90,
Aspen,
Colorado 81612,
USA
Tel: (303) 925 3742

Bluebird Manufacturing Inc.,
PO Box 2307,
Fort Collins,
Colorado 80522
USA
Tel: (303) 484 3243

Pug Mills

Bluebird Manufacturing Inc.,
(as above)

Venco Products,
2, Kilburn Way,
Kelmscott,
West Australia 6111,
Australia
Tel: (09) 399 5265

Potterycrafts Ltd.,
Campbell Road,
Stoke-on-Trent,
Staffordshire ST4 4ET,
England
Tel: (0782) 272 2444

Jaimen Mechanical Engineers,
Busia Road,
PO Box 18200,
Nairobi
Tel: 556 474

www.ingramcontent.com/pod-product-compliance
Ingram Content Group UK Ltd.
Pitfield, Milton Keynes, MK11 3LW, UK
UKHW050457150426
5217IPUK00025B/1723